國立公園
日光の展望

復刻版

柏田 健介【編】

PICTORIAL
NIKKO NATIONAL PARK

随想舎

FOREWORD

"Do not say the word *Kekko* (magnificent) until you have seen *Nikko*." So goes a saying. We do not think it necessary to tell that Nikko—which is a substitute for the word "magnificent," according to the above saying,—is truly worthy of boasting itself to the whole world on the splendour of its structures built with extreme extravagance and its elaborate works of arts done in their essence.

The beauty of Nikko, however, does not consist merely in the artificial beauty of the structures, but also in the natural beauty of water, mountains, lakes, etc.; these two combined in beautiful harmony make Nikko a great paradise on earth. This is the very reason why it makes so much noise in the world as the representative park of Japan.

There are many requirements for parks to be specified as "the national parks," but they can be summed up into three points; that is, they contribute to the health, recreation and culture of the nation with the surroundings of their beautiful scenery, which, when edified to their perfection, ought to shine brilliantly upon the whole world.

From this point of view, Nikko has an absolute supremacy over any other parks in Japan; it is second to none in the beauty of arts and nature: there is not an edifice, nor a tree, nor a stone but seems to have got something divine emanated from *Futara-Kami*, its guardian god; there is no other park which has such rich and abundant life and substance as Nikko does.

"**The Outline of Nikko**" has been compiled with a view to introducing all these aspects of Nikko collected in a single volume. There were already published a superabundance of albums and books concerning Nikko, but most of them were merely partial guide-books and were too insufficient to show the whole Nikko as a national park of Japan.

With this point in view, we have tried to avoid falling a prey to such a near-sighted prejudice as is often found in the so-called *Meisho-zue*, "the pictures of fine sights," but to make it a perfect illustrated book containing every aspect of the whole Nikko. In order, accordingly, to show it from every angle, in edifices, mountains, rivers, valleys, lakes, watering places, etc., we have tried to leave no stone unturned for the purpose, introducing everything and all interesting, from the grand sights of the inner Nikko even to those of the *Kinu* Gorge, not to say of the magnificent structures of *Toshogu* and *Daiyubyo* as well as the famous lakes and waterfalls such as *Chuzenji*, *Kegon* and so forth. And in the reproduction of the photogravure we have paid a special attention to the variety of objects, treating them from polygonal view-points, and tried as much as possible to avoid such a cut and dried composition as is often found.

Of course we do not think this to be a perfect thing,—far from it,—we admit it necessitates many readjustments; yet we feel sure that this book will make a good guide and companion to those who are yet to come, and a pleasant souvenir to those who had the happiness of visiting it already.

はしがき

「日光を見ずして結構といふ勿れ」といふ言葉がある。それほどに豪華壯麗の代名詞となつてゐる日光――その贅美の限りをつくした建築物の絢爛、美術工藝の精粹は正に全世界に誇るべきものであること茲に事新らしく論ずるまでもない。

而して、日光の美なるものは單に人工の極致を示した建築物の壯麗に止まらず、更に山と水との自然景觀を加へて天衣無縫の一大樂園たらしめたところに眞の結構がある。これ即ち、本邦國立公園中の代表的風光として喧傳されつゝある所以であらねばならぬ。

由來、國立公園としての要求はいろ〳〵あるにしても、要するに、明媚なる風景を中心として、保健・休養・敎化の三點に約まり、それが國家的のものとして全面的に解放されて光を放つところに國立公園の眞面目がある。この點から日光を見ると斷じて他の追隨を許さぬ優越を有ち、その山と水と建築美とは天下に四儔を見ず、全山にわたる一木一草にも二荒神の偉大なる神格が搖曳してゐる。これほどに內部生命の豐かな存在が又とあらうか。

「日光展望」は、これらの全貌を一瞬にあつめて其景觀を紹介せんが爲に編んだもので、從來、日光に關する寫眞帳や案內書の類は所謂、汗牛充棟もたゞならぬほど多分に刊行されてゐるが、その多くが局部的な案內書たるに止まり、眞に國立公園日光の全貌を窺ふべく頗る物足りなさを感ぜしめたことは遺憾であつた。

本書は特に此點に意を用ゐ、所謂名所圖繪式、近視眼的偏見に墮するの弊を避け、飽く迄も全日光の景觀悉くを蒐集して一大圖錄たらんことを念願としたものである。

即ち建築物に、山岳に、河川に、谿谷に、湖沼に、泉鄕に、あらゆる角度より全日光の景觀を展望せしめるため、東照宮・大猷廟等の豪華はもとより、中禪寺湖・華嚴瀧其他名瀑名湖の紹介をはじめ、日光群峰の壯觀より奧日光・鬼怒溪谷に至るまで、その全貌を捉へて萬遺憾なきを期し、寫眞製版等の複製にあたりても、對象の變化を尊重し、多角的の視野によつて之を取扱ひ、在來の無味乾燥なる構圖は努めてこれを避けた事等、いさゝか苦心の存するところを敢て自負するものである。

もとより是をもつて理想的の日光展望となすは當らず、尚幾多再吟味の要あること勿論であるが、或ひは遊覽の參考に、或ひは曾遊の記念として大方諸賢の好伴侶ともなれば望外の幸甚である。

[凡例]
本書は、柏田健介氏所蔵の、昭和10年3月10日発行『國立公園 日光の展望』（発行所 星野屋分店／編集兼発行者 柏田長七／印刷所 下野美術工藝社）を復刻したものである。しかし、編集制作の都合上、折り込み地図を巻頭におき、新たに別丁扉を設けた。また、製本、用紙など復刻が困難な工程は簡略化した。凡例および巻末の解説は、復刻に際し付け加えたものである。

CONTENTS

THE EXTREMITY OF MAGNIFICENCE 1	THROUGH THE VALLEY 23
THE AVENUE RECALLING THE PAST 2	ROARING WITH THE SACRED RHYTHM 24
THE SACRED BRIDGE............. 3	INTERESTING WITH DIFFERENT ASPECTS 25
THE LIGHT OF TRUTH GLITTERS .. 4	WATERFALLS 26
INTO THE SACRED GROUNDS 5	A CALM MORNING 27
TOWERING ABOVE THE SACRED WOODS........................ 6	LAKE CHUZENJI 28
TREASURES 7	THE BRIDGE AT THE LAKE-TAIL .. 29
EVER BRILLIANT 8	KANNON-DO 30
IN THE PRECINCTS 9	BOATING ON THE LAKE 31
LOOK UP AT THE SPLENDOUR!.... 10	THE RAPIDS 32
THE ESSENCE OF ARTS 11	FULL OF POETRY 33
THE ESSENCE OF RESPLENDENCY 12	A SPA ON THE LAKE-SIDE 34
THE HOLY OF HOLIES............ 13	A SEQUESTERED NOOK 35
RECALLING THE PAST............ 14	ON THE MOUNTAIN TOP......... 36
THE GUARDIAN GOD OF THE SACRED REGION 15	FROM THE PASS 37
THROUGH THE GATES 16	LAKES 38
BESIDE THE FOREFATHER'S MAUSOLEUM 17	THE HOT SPRINGS............. 39
WONDERING AT THE GORGEOUSNESS 18	THE FAIRYLAND............... 40
INTO THE MAUSOLEUM 19	IF WINTER COMES............. 41
NEVER TIRED 20	FRAGRANCE IN THE SACRED REGION 42
UP LIKE A WIND................ 21	THE GORGE................... 43
THE MAGNIFICENT VIEW OF WATER AND MOUNTAIN........ 22	THE CHARM OF THE SPA 44
	ROWING IN THE CLEAR STREAM .. 45
	EVER SURPRISED 46
	THE AUTUMN TINTS IN A FAIRYLAND 47

目 次

□	廟門をくぐりて ……… 16	岩角に激しつゝ ……… 32
豪華の極み ……… 1	祖廟に並ぶ ……… 17	詩情溢るゝ ……… 33
懐古の並樹 ……… 2	華麗に睹る ……… 18	湖畔に湧く ……… 34
朱欄美はしく ……… 3	廟内深く ……… 19	幽邃に描く ……… 35
法燈は煌く ……… 4	訪ね行けば ……… 20	頂に立てば ……… 36
神域に入る ……… 5	風の如く登る ……… 21	峠を辿る ……… 37
神林を抽く ……… 6	見晴かす山水美 ……… 22	沼に題す ……… 38
み寶を秘めて ……… 7	谿を辿りて ……… 23	湯の香慕ひて ……… 39
千古麗はしく ……… 8	神韻を籠めて ……… 24	神秘の仙境 ……… 40
境内に見る ……… 9	興趣限りなく ……… 25	冬来りなば ……… 41
壯麗を仰ぐ ……… 10	瀑布に見る ……… 26	聖域に香る ……… 42
偉靈に額づく ……… 11	靜かなる朝 ……… 27	蒼水淳々 ……… 43
絢爛の精 ……… 12	湖上を航る ……… 28	泉郷の王座 ……… 44
靈廟を拜す ……… 13	湖尻に架る ……… 29	清流に漕ぐ ……… 45
古を偲ぶ ……… 14	觀音堂に詣でゝは ……… 30	迎接に違なく ……… 46
靈域の鎭護 ……… 15	船を泛べて ……… 31	仙境に彩る ……… 47

THE EXTREMITY OF MAGNIFICENCE

ikko, with its natural beauty and artificial magnificence, is truly a grand sight worth to be praised as the quintessence of our national parks. It always comes to the top among the famous sights of Japan, when they are to be introduced to the world.

To begin with, Nikko might truly be called the essence of the natural beauty of Japan, with the grandness of its mountains, the clearness of its streams, the calmness of its lakes, and the mightiness of its waterfalls; with the rich foliage of trees and the beautiful tints of autumn leaves; in short, with every variety of views gathered in a single place.

To make it more, there are the gloriously magnificent structures, the very essence of our arts with their everlasting life and radiance, and **Yomei-mon** above all, the extremity of magnificence, worthy of the highest eulogy, "Never speak the word *Kekko* (magnificent) until you have seen *Nikko*," and known to every nook and corner of our country.

Indeed, it may well be called a great paradise on earth.

How great is Nikko!

NIKKO NATIONAL PARK

豪華の極み

天然の美、人工の麗、日光こそはわが國立公園の粹を誇るべき一大景觀であり、輝ける日本の名勝として世界に紹介される時、必ずや第一指に屈せらるべきであらう。

まことに東照宮の豪壯華麗にして就中、陽明門の如き所謂「日光を見ずして結構といふなかれ」といふ最上級の禮讚によつて津々浦々まで普及されてゐるところ、山岳美の壯大雄美、溪流の淸冽、湖沼の幽玄等々相まつて眞に神山靈蹟の名に背かず、二荒の神の鎭まりますところ、關八州の主神として仰がれ、遙かにつゞく野の遠近、若葉照り、紅葉輝き、大小の湖沼は眸をうるませて神秘の謎をたゝへ、溪谷のおもむくところ、流れてはせゝらぎの靜寂に、墜ちては瀑布の壯觀など、日光群峰をめぐる變化に富める景觀美はまさに日本風景美のエッセンスでなくてなんであらう。

絢爛目を奪ふ建築物の豪華版にいたつては我國美術工藝の精華として光彩陸離たるものがある。至上至高、藝術の香の匂ふところ、千古不滅の生命を展開してゐる。黑髮の嶺高く、大谷の流澄むところ、永遠に一大樂園として世界景觀史上に重きをなすであらう。

偉大なる哉、日光よ。

YOMEI-MON
陽明門

み極の華豪
The extremity of gorgeousness.

THE AVENUE RECALLING THE PAST

he cryptomeria avenue plays the prelude to the grand sights of Nikko. What is generally called Nikko consists of shrines, temples and other structures as well as the beautiful scenery of water and mountains, all found in the river range of the *Daiya* between the mountain ranges of *Nikko* and *Ashio*.

Nikko can be reached by various ways, but the most impressive is the avenue along which tens of thousands of old cryptomerias grow, towering very high and making it dark and gloomy even in the daytime.

These trees were planted by *Masatsuna Matsudaira, the daimyo of Kawagoe*, one of the commissioners in charge of the construction of *Toshogu* about three hundred years ago.

The avenue, beginning near *Toshogu*, extends as far as *Taun* where it divides itself into three—the ways to *Kanuma*, *Aizu* and *Utsunomiya*, each having the avenue more than five miles; the avenues, the greatest of all the avenues of the world, extend more than twenty-two miles in all; and the old trees numbering about 20,000 amount to a million yen at the current price.

In those days, most of the feudal lords rushed to dedicate to Toshogu *torii*, standing lanterns and the like, while *Masatsuna* alone dedicated these plants, though laughed at by some, which must be said to have been a capital idea looking forward to hundreds of years afterwards. Those who pay a visit to Nikko are first impressed by its overpowering dignity.

NIKKO NATIONAL PARK

懐古の並樹

日光の景観中その前奏曲はまづ杉並木の莊嚴美に始まる。一般にいはゆる日光と稱するのは日光火山群と足尾山塊との間に挾まれた大谷川を東から奧へ溯つた流域にあるところの社寺と其の建築物、及び山水の景致が主體であり、各方面から幾筋もの街道が通じてゐるが、蠱々として天空に聳え立つてゐる幾萬本の杉並木は晝なほ暗い莊嚴のうちに、まづ參者の襟を正さしめる。

此の杉並木は今を距ること三百餘年前、東照宮造營總奉行の一人であつた川越の城主、松平正綱が二十有餘年の辛苦を經て栽植の上寄進したもので、まづ東照宮附近におとり今市にいたつて三道にわかれ、鹿沼街道は三里十五丁又挾の彼方にいたり、宇都宮街道及び會津街道は各二里十六丁にわたり延長約十里の間に現存する老樹約二萬本に及び時價百萬圓に近く世界唯一の大並木とされてゐる。

現に史蹟として指定されてゐるが、當時、大小名の多くが競つて鳥居や燈籠を寄進した中に千載の後圖を案じて杉並木に着眼したことは、まさに時流を拔く卓識である。正綱の遠謀深慮より今日の一大壯觀を遺した偉功は沒却することができない。

けだし天下の偉觀として日光神域を踏むものにとつては第一印象として、まづかぎりなき森嚴の氣に打たれるであらう。

THE SACRED BRIDGE

A vermillion bridge sharply relieved against the dark green of the woods —what a beautiful contrast! It is called the **Sacred Bridge** or **God's Bridge** of Nikko.

With the clear stream of the *Daiya* flowing under it, and the graceful mountain towering behind, the bridge, sharply outlined among the green leaves, or mingled among the tinted leaves of autumn, or bound in silver snow in winter, has something divine about it. It is about 90 feet long with ten railing posts ornamented at the tops, and is painted vermillion. Both ends of the bridge are blocked with wood palisades, prohibiting anyone except the Imperial messengers to cross it.

A legend goes about the bridge. About 1,200 years ago, when *Dosho-shonin*, a virtuous priest and the original founder of Nikko, was travelling on a pilgrimage through the country, he came on the river (*Daiya*) but could not cross it, so deep and rapid was the water at the time. So he prayed and prayed and lo! there appeared to him a sacred vision of *Shinsa*, a Buddhist god, who let go two snakes from his hands, which became a bridge, and he could easily go across the river. Hence it is also called a **snake bridge**.

It is the very symbol of Nikko.

NIKKO NATIONAL PARK

朱欄美はしく

滴らんとする翠色に朱塗の橋のかゝるところ、對照の妙を得て眼のさめるやうな美しさ、日光の**神橋**こそはまさに其の極致を描いてあまりますところがない。

大谷川の清流を脚下に、しかも秀麗なる山岳を背景とするところ、若葉に紅葉に、ましてや雪の景色ともなれば、その神々しくも又嚴肅なる風景は拜するものをして等しく肅然として襟を正さしめるものがある。

橋は長さ十五間三尺、擬寶珠十基、その柱は徑一尺六寸、欄干橋板ともに總朱塗、金具はすべて鍍金の獅子彫、橋柱は四本の巨岩を削つて造り橋頭には朱塗の木柵を設け、平時はこれを鎖して庶人の通行を許さない。

今より一千百五十餘年前、日光山の開祖勝道上人がはじめて此の場所へ來た時、折惡しく絶涯深く流れ漲つて渡ることができないので専念神佛に祈誓したところ、不思議や深沙大王の尊容があり〲と顯はれ、手にした青と赤の兩蛇を放つと見ゆるやたちまち一條の橋と化し、しかも山菅を生じたので易々としてこれを渡ることを得たといふ傳説があり、山菅橋又は蛇橋とも稱へられたのが此橋の創始である。

大日光の象徴(シンボル)として憧れの目標であることは世界人の等しく認めるところであらう。

THE LIGHT OF TRUTH GLITTERS

There is a cylindrical copper column, about 45 feet high, near the *Rinnoji* Temple. It is called **Sorinto**, "the Evil Averting Pillar."

In the ancient time, *Dengyo-Daishi*, the founder of *Tendai* sect, erected such pillars at six places in our country, beginning with *Mt. Hiei*, in order to drive evils out of Japan.

Priest *Tenkai*, *Jigen-Daishi* by posthumous name, followed the ancient sage and erected one at Nikko about three hundred years ago. It was formerly erected on the mountain near the inner shrine of *Toshogu*, but was removed to the present site.

It is about nine feet in circumference, and has twenty-seven "*yoraku*" (something like a necklace) and twenty-four gold bells near the top, and two crests of hollyhock (the *Tokugawas*' family crest) with 64 verses quoted from *Dengyo-Daishi* carved on it below the head decorations. The gold glitters bright even now as the symbol of the religious light.

Shiimeshi—shiki, "the ceremony of pressing one to eat rice," is famous from of old and quite unique. It is also called *Nikko-Zeme*, "the Nikko Torture." In old days, it was done on New Year's Day and at April Festival, but now on the evening of Jan. 2 at *Sambutsudo*.

Sambutsudo is the biggest structure in Nikko, about 108 feet wide, 84 feet deep and 138 feet high, with a roof of copper tiles and painted vermillion. Formerly it was near the *Futarasan* shrine, but was moved to the present site. It is now used as the principal hall of the *Rinnoji* Temple. It has the sitting images of *Amida-Nyorai*, *Senju-Kannon* and *Bato-Kannon* together with those of *Jikei-Daishi* and *Jigen Daishi*. There is an old cherry-tree called *Kongo--sakura*, very famous, in front of the hall.

NIKKO NATIONAL PARK

法燈は煌く

天空高く煌きわたる四丈八尺の法燈、名づけて相輪塔といふ。古、天台宗の開祖傳教大師が比叡山を初め、日本國内六ケ所に建立したものに擬し天海僧正即ち慈眼大師が建立したものである。

當初、東照宮奥の院の山にあつたが慶安三年二荒山新宮の傍に移し、その後更に明治八年現在の地に移轉した。廻り九尺五寸、上に滅金瓔珞二十七箇金鈴二十四をつるし、下部に葵の金紋二個を付し傳教大師の願文に摸して六十四句を刻し、風伯雨師もこれを蝕することを能はず、今尙金色燦然として光を放つてゐる。

日光の強飯式は昔から名高く且つ珍らしいものとされてゐる。文字通り飯を強ゆるの儀で世にこれを日光責と稱し、舊幕時代には毎年四月の祭禮の外、正月には本坊で行はれたが、現今は正月二日夜三佛堂內で行はれてゐる。

三佛堂は日光第一の大建築物で間口十八間、奥行十四間、高さ二十三間の銅瓦總朱塗、明治九年までは相輪塔とともに二荒山神社の傍にあつたが今は輪王寺の本堂となり、內堂に阿彌陀如來・千手觀音・馬頭觀音及慈惠慈眼兩大師像を安置し每月の寒日には參拜者雲集して雜沓する。堂前の老櫻は金剛櫻と稱へて名高く陽春萬朶の花を咲かせる。

[4]

SAMBUTSUDO, NIKKO
日光三佛堂

THE SORIN TOWER
相輪塔

法燈は煌く
The glimmering light of religion.

GOHAN-SHIKI, AN OLD CEREMONY, AT NIKKO
日光山、古式强飯式

GOHAN-SHIKI, AN OLD CEREMONY, AT NIKKO
日光山、古式强飯式

INTO THE SACRED GROUNDS

oshogu, with the rank of *Bekkaku Kampeisha*, "a special government shrine", makes the very centre of Nikko scenery. Its edifices and artificial works are nothing but divine works and show the very prestige of great *Iyeyasu* who was deified as *Tosho-Daigongen* after his death.

On entering the sacred grounds, you will find old cryptomerias towering high with their thick foliage. Presently you will come to a stone pillar, on which is inscribed "*Toshogu, Bekkaku-Kampeisha.*" This is the very front of the shrine *Toshogu*. A divine atmosphere reigns all around.

Needless to say, *Toshogu* is the mausoleum of **Iyeyasu Tokugawa,** of *Sho-ichii* (the senior first rank at court), *Dajo-Daijin* (the prime minister), *Seii-Tai-shogun* (the chief commander of the force). The grounds have 27,000 *tsubo* (about two and a quarter English acres) in area.

The present mausoleum was rebuilt in 1624 and took 13 years to complete it; its luxuriant edifices are the very specimens of the structure of Tokugawa Period.

It was posthumously conferred the Senior First Rank from the court in 1617, granted the name "Toshogu" in 1645, and ranked as the special government shrine in 1873.

The lower plate shows **a revolving lantern,** 12 feet high, made of yellow copper, in nonagon with snake-posts at the corners, with iron nets around and a copper support at the centre and 5 supports in each of two tiers. It was dedicated from Korea but was made at Nagasaki by a Dutch, so that it has something of an European style, and the crest of hollyhock has been put upside down by mistake.

NIKKO NATIONAL PARK

THE FRONT OF TOSHOGU
東照宮社頭

神域に入る
Coming into the sacred compounds.

THE REVOLVING LANTERN
廻り燈篭

TOWERING ABOVE THE SACRED WOODS

The structures of *Toshogu* are all very beautiful and magnificent, but above all, **the five storeyed tower** spiring above the rich foliage of old cryptomerias gives an exquisite taste to the beauty of the precincts with its symmetrical gracefulness. It was dedicated by *Tadakatsu Sakai, Daimyo of Kohama*, in 1650, but was burned down in 1815 and rebuilt. It is 116 feet high, the lowest storey being 18 feet square; all painted vermillion, though its inside is painted in gorgeous colours, and roofed with copper tiles; every storey has doors on four sides, and the posts are covered with gold brocades and have carvings of 12 zodiacal animals.

The principal image is *Gochi-Nyorai*, and the images of *Jikokuten, Zochoten, Komokuten* and *Bishamonten* are also placed.

On the right of the stone-steps, within a stone-fence, is a big stone called "*Abomaru*," and on the left is also one called "*Suberimo-ishi*."

NIKKO NATIONAL PARK

神林を抽く

東照宮諸建築の景觀はいづれも結構壯麗の極みであるが、わけても亭々たる神代ながらの老杉の梢を抽いて、雲表高く聳立する**五重塔**の端正と壯麗はその白眉で、境內に無上の風趣を添へてゐる。

この塔は慶安三年小濱城主酒井讚岐守忠勝の寄進にかゝり、文化十二年火を失して烏有に歸し、其後再建されたものであるが、高さ十一丈六尺、下層は三間四方、總朱塗、銅瓦葺、桝組みで、內陣に壯麗の彩色を施し、各層四面に黑塗の扉があり、柱は全部金襴卷で、上部に美事なる十二支が彫刻されてゐる。

本尊は五智如來で、外に持國天・增長天・廣目天・毘沙門天を安置し、石階の右方、石垣の中に阿房丸、同左方に滑海藻石と稱へる巨石がある。

神林を抽く
The sacred wood.

THE FIVE-STORIED PAGODA
五重塔

TREASURES

he great range of sights in Nikko is itself a national treasure as a park, but most of the edifices are specified as the national treasures by the state and are made much of in the history of the Japanese fine arts.

The **snow view** in front of the guard-house, for instance, is an example of nature and art put together in harmonious contrast. The glorious edifice on one side and the snow symbolizing purity and quietness on the other—the exquisite contrast is beyond description.

Again, the **carving of three monkeys** in the transom window above the beam in the sacred stable is as famous as that of the sleeping cat in *Sakashita-mon*. They illustrate the precept, "Neither see, hear, nor speak any evil." It is quite a masterpiece. It is said to have been put there according to a tradition of monkeys and the horse disease. The sacred stable was built in the style of *nagare-zukuri*, roofed with copper tiles, and using plain wood.

Near the stable towers a big umbrella-pine tree (*Koyamaki*), of which *Iyeyasu* was very fond. It was planted by *Iyemitsu*, the third Shogun, himself. A tradition tells that it was brought from *Koyasan* by *Kobo-daishi* (a virtuous priest about 1100 years ago) when it was a young shoot, and *Iyemitsu* transplanted it to the present place.

NIKKO NATIONAL PARK

み寶を秘めて

日光群峰をめぐる一大景觀は、蓋し代表的國立公園として國寶的な大自然であると同時に、壯麗無比藝術の極致を示す建築物の大部分は又と得難き國寶で、本邦美術工藝史上實に重きをなすものである。たとへば境内番所前に見る雪景のごとき、大自然の美しさと人工の美との調和がいかに對照の妙を極めてゐるかの一例で、絢爛眼を奪ふ豪華な建築物と、靜寂そのもののやうな神域に降り積む雪景色とによつて釀し出される微妙な美しさは、まことに形容の言葉を超越した國寶的風景である。

三猿彫刻は有名な眠り猫と共に並び稱されるもので御神厩長押上の欄間にあり、所謂、見ざる聞かざる言はざるを諷した有名な作品で、寫形構想ともに實に見事な傑作であり、猿と馬疫に關する傳説に基き制作されたものと稱されてゐる。

御神厩は流造、屋根銅瓦木葺、軒裏と建具は蠟色塗、他は總て素木造りで、傍に亭々と繁り立つ金松樹は東照神君御好みの樹とあり、三代將軍家光公が手づから植ゑたもので周圍一丈に餘り、弘法大師が紀州高野山より移した若木を更に移植したものである。

みを秘めて
The treasures.

THREE MONKEYS, SYMBOLIZING "NEVER SEE, NOR HEAR, NOR SPEAK EVIL OF OTHERS"
三猿

THE SNOW VIEW IN FRONT OF THE GUARD-HOUSE
境内番所前の雪景

THE STABLE OF TOSHOGU
東照宮御廐

EVER BRILLIANT

omei-mon, "the Brilliant Gate," which can be looked up from the front yard of *Toshogu*, was crowned by the ancients with the highest eulogy of *Higurashi-mon*, "the gate where one tarries all day long," but as a modern view it is equally magnificent in contrast and harmony with its surroundings.

With a big *torii* standing on the clean gravels in the centre of the yard, then a flight of stone steps with standing lanterns on each side, and the stone fence guarding the terrace, the brilliant gate stands out in relief with its bright colours against the background of the dark-green foliage behind. The symmetrical harmony of all these will strike you with a sense of noble magnificence.

On the right of the front gate stand three structures in a row; they are the sacred godowns, which are said to have cost about 800,000 yen at the current price. They were built in "*azekura*" style, with roofs of copper tiles, and are painted in gorgeous colours.

One of them has a carving of an elephant under the gable, a very famous work, the design of which was done by *Tanyu Kano*, a well-known painter.

NIKKO NATIONAL PARK

千古麗はしく

東照宮の前庭に立つて望む陽明門は、昔の人が所謂「日暮門」として最上級の讚辭を呈した以外に、近代的な景觀としても對照調和の妙を極めた畫面である。大鳥居を中心として、塵一つだに止めぬ玉川砂利の彼方、石燈籠・玉垣・石段の清淨なる——老杉の木蔭、鬱蒼たる森を背景に浮び出でたる陽明門の端麗なる——その構圖と配色の妙と相俟つて眞に恍惚去る能はざらしめるものがあり、その壯嚴美は我を忘れしめるであらう。

表門に隣して右に三棟連つてゐるのが神庫で、下神庫・中神庫・上神庫と呼ばれ、この三神庫の造營費は今日の時價に換算して約七十八萬七千餘圓と稱へられてゐる。いづれも桁行約九間から十二間、梁間三間乃至四間餘、皆校倉造り、銅瓦葺・總朱塗・花鳥草木の極彩色で、柱上は金襴卷、一庫每に扉が二つあり、上神庫の外長押上には大きさ五尺ばかりの大象の彫刻があるが下繪は狩野探幽で、技神に入つて最も有名である。下神庫の背後にある朱塗りの齊淨は間口五間、奥行五尺、佛家七堂伽藍の一つで厠であるなどいかにも日光らしい。

THE FRONT YARD OF TOSHOGU
東照宮前庭

千古麗はしく
The everlasting beauty.

THE THREE STORES, TOSHOGU.
東照宮三神庫

IN THE PRECINCTS

mizuya, "The Water-House," dedicated by *Katsushige Nabeshima*, Lord of *Shinano*, is a tiny house with three granite pillars, ten feet high, at each corner; there is a painted carving of a dragon among the waves, under the gable. Clear and pure water is always gushing out of the granite cistern.

Rindo, a two storeyed edifice, is 36 feet square and 40 feet high. The inside is paved, in the centre of which is *Rinzo* in which is treasured *Issaikyo,* "the whole collection of sutras,"

In front of *Rindo*, under the stone fence, there are two standing iron lanterns, very famous, dedicated by *Masamune Date*, one of the biggest *Daimyo*, who is said to have made them moulded, spending three years' tax in his big domain.

Tobikoe-jishi, "the Jumping Lion," carved on one of the stone posts in front of Yomei-mon, was done by *Tsukudayu*, the famous engraver of *Saidaiji*, *Bizen*; when *Iyemitsu*, the third Shogun, saw it, he was much pleased with it, and so it is also called "the Lion of Pleasure."

Yakushido is a beautiful temple painted vermillion, and full of antiqueness. The principal image was brought from *Horaiji* Temple in the province of *Mikawa*. On the ceiling of the nave is painted a big dragon in black by *Tanyu Kano*. If you clap your hands under the dragon's head, you will hear a creaking sound; hence it is called "a Creaking Dragon." Again, as there is no cloud about it, it is also called "a Naked Dragon."

境内に見る
In the precinct.

THE CISTERN OF TOSHOGU
東照宮御水舎

RINDO
輪堂

THE JAMPING LION
子眠の獅子

YAKUSHIDO
薬師堂

THE CREAKING DRAGON
鳴龍

LOOK UP AT THE SPLENDOUR !

he most famous structure in Nikko, **Yomei-mon**, "the Radiant Gate," is popularly called *Higurashi-mon*, "the gate where one tarries all day long," because one can spend a whole day, admiring and wondering at its gorgeous splendour. It is perhaps the most resplendent structure ever constructed by Japanese craftsmen of olden days. The name *Yomei* was granted by the court and the framed tablet held up in front was written by the Emperor *Gomizunoo* himself; hence another name, "the Imperial Tablet Gate." It is gorgeously decorated with a wealth of elaborated fittings and carvings; the carvings of blessed birds and flowers, sacred animals and dragons, and of famous heroes and statesmen in the chinese legends, most of which are gorgeously painted in bright colours. And there are also paintings on the ceilings, done by the first rate artists in those days, among which the rising dragon painted by *Tanyu Kano* is the most famous.

This gate, together with other *Toshogū* buildings, was constructed by the third Shogun in memory of his grandfather *Iyeyasu*. It is estimated that the gate alone cost about 1,200,000 yen at the current price.

Visitors can always appreciate its variegated beauty through the year round.

NIKKO NATIONAL PARK

壯麗を仰ぐ

俗に「日暮門」と稱へてポピュラーの存在となつてゐる陽明門は本邦建築物中、絢爛豪華の代表で陽明の號は畏くも朝廷より賜り、正面上に揭げる東照大權現の額は後水尾天皇の御宸筆であるので「勅額門」とも稱へられてゐる。

天井の畫龍は狩野探幽の筆、精巧を極めたその柱は彫刻彩色の妙をつくし、此門だけで時價約百二十萬圓を要したといふから世界無比ともいふべく人工の極致を示す處正に驚異そのものである。

而も、その壯嚴さは四時の風物に伴ひ千變萬化の美しさを見せ、たとへば、春の曙、霞の中に浮ぶ極彩色の美しさ、靑葉若葉の夏ともなれば建築美に照り映ゆる白い光の中に古代藝術の光輝燦然たるものがあり、「あら尊と靑葉若葉に日の光」と詠んだ芭蕉の心持が偲ばれてあまりがある。紅葉黄葉、滿山に錦を織りなす秋は嚴肅の氣神域に充ち滿ち、常磐樹に點綴する紅葉黄葉の美は、壯麗の建物に反映してまことに一幅の畫である。

ましてや、冬の雪景色に至つては全く淸淨そのもので、燈籠に、屋根に、大鳥居に、玉垣に、石段に、老杉の梢に、たわゝに積る白雪に、たゞみる白銀の世界は絢爛たる建築物と融合して一層配色の美を發揮してゐる。

[10]

YOMEIMON
陽明門

壮麗を仰ぐ
Looking up the splendour

BEAUTIFULLY DECORATED BY SNOW
雪の装ひ麗しく

THE ESSENCE OF ARTS

e do not need to tell that *Yomei-mon* is the highest marvel in the whole Nikko. Passing through the gate, you will come to **Kara-mon,** "the Chinese gate," with gables in the Chinese style.

On the front beam are to be seen the bronze beasts called "*Tsutsuga-no-mushi*," and on the roof ridge two bronze dragons. The front pillars have each a rising or a falling dragon. Under the roof and gables, on the ceiling and pillars, there are many engravings on the chinese precious wood, the subjects all taken from the Chinese history or legends; hence the name of the gate.

This gate, together with the Back *Kara-mon* and the West *Kara-mon,* and with the roofed fence, encloses in them *Haiden,* "the Oratory," and *Honden,* "the Main Chapel." The roofed fence is more than 500 feet long, and is decorated with many carvings on the panels, transom windows and *kekomi*. All these works, together with those of *Yomei-mon* and the corridor, are masterpieces into which the celebrated artists of the day put their heart.

NIKKO NATIONAL PARK

偉靈に額づく

陽明門の壯麗さは全日光の精華であり絶讃であることは今更多言を要しない。門を入ると正面にあるのが唐門である。

唐門は桁行一丈、梁間六尺三寸の唐破風造り、正面棟上には俗に恙の虫といふ獅子に似た銅製の異獸を載せ、東西の棟上に同じく銅製の龍を載せてゐる。又正面左右の柱には昇り龍・降り龍・幣軸に梅竹の寄木高彫り、扉羽目に牡丹梅竹の寄彫り、上部鞘形透し、天井の欅一枚板には彈琴天人、破風下に巢父許由、後部に浪と兎、四方の臺輪上に堯帝、七賢人、七福人の彫刻があるが、いづれも諸種の唐木を寄せて作つたもの、唐門の名ある所以である。

門の左右に連なる瑞垣は後唐門、西唐門を繋いで拜殿本殿を圍んでゐるが、その延長八十七間、柱は黑塗、羽目は地紋透し彫、上の欄間に華麗なる花木山禽、下の蹴込に淡雅なる水草水禽を彫つてゐる。いづれも雨面籠彫りで、精巧細緻、陽明門廻廊の彫刻と共に名工名匠が一世一代の心血をそゝいだ傑作で、世界に誇るべき我が美術工藝の精粹である。

THE KARAMON AND THE
HONDEN OF TOSHOGU
東照宮唐門及本社

偉靈に額づく
Praying before the great soul.

THE CARVINGS OF
THE CORRIDOR
廻廊彫刻

THE CARVINGS OF YOMEIMON
陽明門の彫刻

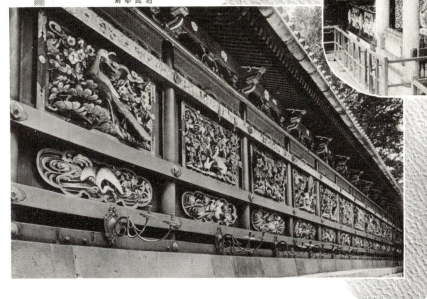

THE ESSENCE OF RESPLENDENCY

Among the structural splendours of *Toshogu*, *Yomeimon* and *Haiden* stand the highest in their arts and beauty. The interior of **Haiden** is divided into three sections. The centre section is a room of worship with a space of 63 mats. In front hangs a bamboo-blind with a big round mirror dedicated by Lord *Tadatomo Sakai*, the then minister. All around the room are carvings and paintings of famous artists. But the most famous are the thirty-six tablets held above the entablatures, in which the Emperor *Gomizunoo* wrote the poems of thirty six sacred poets, while *Mitsuoki Tosa* painted their portraits. The paintings on the screens in west and east are the works of *Tanyu Kano*.

The East Hall is a room for *Shogun* and *Gosanké* (the three branch families of the Togugawas) to sit.

The West Hall is one for *Monshu* (the highest priest) and the administrative ministers to sit.

In both of these halls are decorations of paintings and carvings gorgeously coloured in black, gold and vermillion.

NIKKO NATIONAL PARK

絢爛の精

東照大權現の建築物はいづれ莊嚴華麗の粹ならざるはないが、陽明門とともに雙璧ともいふべきは拜殿の結構でありまさに絢爛の精とも謂ひつべきであらう。

其内部は殿内を三つに區分し中央は即ち
禮拜の間で六十三疊、正面に翠簾を垂れ、酒井忠朝奉獻の直徑二尺五寸の大鏡を揭げ、下には勅使捧進の金幣を立て・ある。柱は總金漆箔極彩色金襴卷、長押上は桐・竹・牡丹・松・梅の花木に鳳凰・孔雀・金鷄・等の極彩色彫物、天井は折上格天井で岩紺靑地に置上彩色の丸龍を畫きいづれも其形狀を異にしてゐる。長押上に揭げられた三十六歌仙扁額の歌は畏くも後水尾天皇の御宸筆にかゝり、畫は土佐光起の筆で、東西襖戶の金泥地に畫いた竹に麒麟・牡丹に狂獅子は狩野探幽の筆である。

東の間は聽聞所と稱へ、將軍及御三家の着座席で上段天井は二重折上造で中央に伽羅の一枚板で葵の小紋を作り、東羽目の彫刻は桐と鳳凰を紫檀・黑檀・鐵刀木等の貴材を寄せて造り、欄間の花鳥桝組には精巧な蒔繪を施してゐる。

西の間は門主及び大臣着座の間で上段天井の中央に絢爛たる極彩色の天人を彫刻し西羽目の彫刻は鷲に松柏の唐木寄木細工をもつてし美術工藝の精華を發揮してゐる。

THE INTERIOR OF THE HAIDEN, TOSHOGU
東照宮拜殿內部

The quintessence of brilliancy.

THE HOLY OF HOLIES

he Sleeping Cat, a skilful carving attributed to the celebrated artist *Hidari* ("Left-handed") *Jingoro*, is so famous that there is no one who comes to Nikko but talks about it. It lies above a side gate on the corridor in front of *Sakashita-mon* which leads to *Okusha*. The cat sleeping in the spring sunshine is so skilfully carved that there has arisen even a legend that by virtue of this cat all the Nikko structures are never damaged by any mouse.

The way to *Okusha* is a long flight of 207 stone steps—each step made of one flag-stone—leading to the sanctuary.

In the Shogunate days, no one was allowed to come near **Okusha**, "the Inner Shrine." Now you can see its *Haiden*, "the Oratory," also full of artistic works on the pillars and ceiling. There are two image dogs dedicated by *Masatsuna Matsudaira* and *Yasutomo Akimoto*.

Behind *Haiden* is a bonze gate with stone fences on each side on a raised terrace, in which is a round bronze pagoda, 11 feet high and 4 feet in diametre. This is the very tomb of *Iyeyasu Tokugawa*, the great hero. The public is not admitted to this Holy of Holies. It is dark here even in the daytime, with the rich foliage of old cryptomerias. It will impress you with a divine feeling.

NIKKO NATIONAL PARK

靈廟を拜す

名匠左甚五郎作と傳へられる眠猫は、苟くも日光を口にするほどの者で知らぬものはないほど有名であるが、東照宮の奥社に達する坂下門前廻廊潛門の蟇股にあるのがそれである。春日陽光を浴びてウツラウツラとしてゐる猫の姿態が迫眞の神技をもつて表現され、此猫あるが爲に日光の廟社は鼠害を被ることがないといふ傳説さへある。

奥宮參道は坂下門より二丁餘、二百七段の石階は奥社の拜殿前まで續き、一段一枚石の贅をつくしてゐる。舊幕時代に參拜を許されなかつた奥社拜殿は南面し、桁行五間三尺、梁間三間二尺、總銅包毛彫模樣があり、格天井に五色の菊花を描いてゐる。前面の白狗二頭は坂下門內唯一の獻品で、松平正綱・秋元泰朝の奉獻である。拜殿背後の石垣上にある唐銅鑄拔門は兩袖に石の瑞垣を廻らし、中に銅製圓形の御寶塔がある。これ即ち英傑德川家康公の墳墓で、直徑四尺、高さ一丈餘、周邊に高く石垣を築き、老杉空を摩して晝尙暗く、神威嚴然としてそゞろに襟を正さしめる。

靈廟を拜す The sanctuary.

THE INUKI-MON AND THE PAGODA ON THE INNER SHRINE, TOSHOGU
東照宮奥宮祓殿叶棟門と寶塔

THE SLEEPING CAT
眠猫

THE MAIN APPROACH TO THE INNER SHRINE
奥宮参道

RECALLING THE PAST

hat recalls to your mind the splendour of the *Tokugawa Shogunate* during the past three hundred years is **the annual festivals** held according to the old customs.

The festivals of Toshogu are well-known throughout the country and attract hundreds of thousands of people and visitors there at the times.

On June 1st, the grand festival day, the Imperial Messengers come from the court and cross the Sacred Bridge, prohibited for any to cross on other days, on the way to the shrine. And the sacred Paranquin, followed by 1,200 inhabitants, each in the old style attire, proceeds through the town as far as the *Futarasan Shrine*, and comes back the next day. Together with the paranquin procession, there is the warriors' procession, also in the ancient warriors' attire.

In the evenings the town people have a folk-dance and they, young and old, dance through the summer nights under the moon shine, celebrating their annual festival. There is another festival held on October 17th, which is less grand than the former one, though it is also popular.

NIKKO NATIONAL PARK

古を偲ぶ

徳川三百年の豪華を今に傳へて當時の榮華を物語るものに古式に則つて行はれるかずぐくの祭典がある。これこそは東照大權現の華であり、日光行事中最も床しい生きた繪卷物である。

東照宮の祭事は昔から名高く殊に神輿行列に至つては他に類例なく毎年拜觀者に賑ひ津々浦々にまで喧傳されてゐる。御祭典のうち、最も有名なのは六月一日の例祭と二日の神輿渡御祭並に十月十七日の渡御祭とで、六月一日には三神輿が二荒山神社に渡御し、二日には二荒山から御旅所へ渡御する。渡御は俗に百物揃ひといひ、昔ながらのいろくくな服裝で千二百餘人の長い行列は日光町其他舊神領町村民が供奉するのが慣しとなつてゐる。

初夏の若葉に照り映ゆるところ、大谷川の水淸く丹塗の色も一際鮮やかに虹と架つた神橋に奉幣使として參向する栃木縣知事の通過は莊嚴にして華麗なる、さながら繪卷物を繰り擴げるの感がある。

神輿行列渡御の比類なき盛觀とその森嚴もさることながら最も床しきは武者行列のかずくくで昔をそのまゝ金紋先箱葵の御紋の御威勢に參道を練るところ、さては月の夜の集ひにさまぐくの裝ひを凝らして短夜を踊り抜く夏祭化裝踊など何れ床しさの限りならざるはない。

THE GUARDIAN GOD OF THE SACRED REGION

he Futarasan Shrine, ranked *Kokuhei Chusha*, is dedicated to three deities; *Onamuji-no-mikoto, Tanarihime-no-mikoto* and *Ajikisukitakahikone-no-mikoto*. More than a thousand years ago, it was first established near the River *Inari* by *Shodo Shonin*, a virtuous priest, but some 670 years ago, it was moved to the present place.

It was worshipped by many emperors since *Kammu-Tenno* and this is the only shrine in Nikko, to which our emperor pays a homage now.

Yayoi-matsuri, "March Festival," is now held from April 13 to 17 every year. Its elegant procession, with hundreds of men beautifully attired in the old style, is said to have no pararell in this country. Spectators, numbering hundreds of thousands, come to see it from far and near.

NIKKO NATIONAL PARK

靈域の鎭護

國幣中社二荒山神社は當初神宮と稱へ日光三社の一であったが維新後本宮、瀧尾、權現の祭神を合祀して**二荒山神社**と稱する事になった。即ち祭神は大巳貴命・田心姫命・味耜高彦根命の三柱である。大同三年勝道上人の勸請で最初稻荷川の畔に祀つてゐたのであるが、度々社地を轉じ今より六百七十年前、即ち建保三年現在の地に社殿を營み今日に至ったので日光開山以來の古社である。現今の社殿は德川氏の初め日光山中興の當時建造したもので桓武天皇を始め歴朝の崇敬篤く、今も日光に於て天皇陛下の御參拜あらせられるのは此の二荒山神社のみであり、いかに神威の尊くして鎮護の大なるものあるかを肯くことができよう。正面の唐銅鳥居は寬政年間の建設で高さ二丈二尺、柱の扁額は有栖川宮熾仁親王殿下の御染筆である。

彌生祭は二荒山神社本社の祭典中、特に世に知られてゐる。古昔は三月二日に行はれたが、明治六年太政官布告によりて四月十七日に改めたもので、祭儀は四月十三日に始まり十七日に終る。その優麗典雅、御行列の諸役數百名に達しその壯麗にして華美なるは全國にその比を絶するものがあり、遠近參拜の群集、實に數萬に及び日光第一の賑ひである。

靈域の鎭護
The guardian deity of the holy land.

THE MARCH FESTIVAL OF FUTARA-SAN
二荒山、彌生祭

THE MARCH FESTIVAL OF FUTARA-SAN
二荒山、彌生祭

國幣中社二荒山神社

THE TORII OF FUTARASAN SHRINE
二荒山神社鳥居

THE HAIDEN OF CHUGUSHI SHRINE
中宮祠拜殿

THROUGH THE GATES

The first gate to *Daiyubyo* is called *Nio-mon*, within which are storehouses, cistern, etc.

A flight of steps leads to **Niten-mon,** the second gate. It is also decorated with many carvings and fittings. The contrast of colours is exquisite. In front above is a framed tablet, the three characters of which, "Daiyubyo," are said to have been written by the Emperor *Gokomyo*.

Within the grates under the gate are set two images of gods, *Komokuten* and *Jikokuten*. But what most attracts the attention of visitors with their life-like freshness are the images of *Fujin* and *Raijin*, "the Wind God and Thunder God," behind the above-mentioned images.

The water-house here is just like that of *Toshogu*; the dragon on the ceiling is the work of *Yasunobu Kano*.

Outside the stone palisade is a big grave stone with two characters, *Kuen*, "Empty Smoke"; it is the tomb of *Abe, Lord of Bungo*, who was buried there according to his will.

NIKKO NATIONAL PARK

廟門をくぐりて

仁天門は三代廟の第二門で東北に面し、梁間五間半、桁行三間半、八脚の樓門造りで、銅瓦葺入母屋、前後軒唐破風、二重扉垂木、組物三手先詰組、前後の破風下に雲と獏、上下層組物の間に牡丹と獅子、波と麒麟等の彫刻があり、木端は獅子頭の丸彫、上部は黒繪塗、下部紅殼塗で、配色の妙得もいはれず、正面に竪六尺餘横四尺餘の扁額があり、大猷院の三文字は後光明天皇の御宸筆と傳へられてゐる。左右の格內には廣目天・持國天の像を安置し、その背後綠朱の色鮮やかに、生々躍動の趣あるのが即ち風神雷神である。

御水舍は東照宮と殆ど同じく、天井の龍は狩野安信の筆、石柵外にある「空煙」の二字を刻した自然石墓碑は阿部豐後守のそれで、遺命に因り此處に葬つたものである。

THE NITEN-MON OF THE
THIRD SHOGUN'S MAUSOLEUM
三代廟二天門

RAIJIN
(THE THUNDER GOD)
雷神

FUJIN
(THE WIND GOD)
風神

廟門をくぐりて
Through the holy gate.

The Karamon (Gate), Sandaibyo Nikko.
THE KARAMON OF THE
THIRD SHOGUN'S MAUSOLEUM
三代廟唐門

THE CISTERN OF THE
THIRD SHOGUN'S MAUSOLEUM
三代廟御水舍

BESIDE THE FOREFATHER'S MAUSOLEUM

aiyubyo, situated beyond the *Futarasan* Shrine, is the mausoleum of *Iyemitsu*, the third *Shogun*, built according to his will, who preferred to be buried near his grandfather. *Daiyubyo*, in the same scale with *Toshogu*, is never inferior to *Toshogu*, though the decoration is not so lavish.

After passing through three gates, you will come to *Kara-mon*, "the chinese-style gate," the main entrance to *Haiden*, "the Oratory," beyond which stands *Honden*, "the Holy Sanctuary," in which is treasured the spirit-tablet of *Iyemitsu*, the third *Shogun*.

Kara-mon of the third Shogun's mansoleum is also in the Chinese style, but the carvings are chiefly of birds and plants, not from the chinese legends as are those of the *Kara-mon* of *Toshogu*.

Haiden is also richly decorated with elaborated carvings of various kinds of sacred birds, beasts and plants.

The twenty-four iron lanterns hanging from the eaves of *Haiden* are the dedication from Lord *Abe Bungo-no-kami*, the then minister.

NIKKO NATIONAL PARK

祖廟に並ぶ

慶安四年四月二十日薨去せられた三代將軍德川家光公の遺命によつて建立された御靈屋三代廟は莊嚴華麗、東照宮に比肩して優劣なく地勢が高い爲却つて幽趣に富んでゐる。

圖は唐門と三代廟拜殿で、唐門は間口一丈三尺餘、大唐破風造で破風下には双鶴、平桁上には金地の波に白龍の彫刻があり木端は獅子頭の圓彫で柱は金卷の丸柱、天井は折揚格天井で格間には極彩色で菊の折枝を彫刻し、門扉は金地に牡丹唐草文は鳳凰を彫つてゐる。左右の袖塀には秋の七草を彫り、是より左右に瑞垣を廻らして拜殿と本殿を圍み、上の欄間には松竹梅花鳥特に群鳩の彫刻を嵌め蹴込には菊唐草の透彫を嵌めてゐる。

門を入れば拜殿で東北に面し桁行十間、梁間四間、入母屋正面千鳥破風向拜軒唐破風附銅葺で二重繁垂組緣勾欄を廻し正面三扉の唐戸には金地に龍獅の彫物を施し其の左右から側面へ押廻して揚蕪(アゲシべ)となつてゐる。向拜の破風下には桐に鳳凰、欄間は松竹梅に鷹の兩面透彫、四本の棟は胡粉摺の角柱で四面には菊と唐草を彫刻してゐる。虹梁は地彫に金箔を置き四方の欄間は百花百鳥の高彫極彩色で檐端には阿部豐後守進獻にかかる釣燈籠二十四光が神々しく垂れ下つてゐる。

THE HAIDEN (ORATORY) OF
THE THIRD SHOGUN'S MAUSOLEUM
三代廟拜殿

祖廟に立ぶ
Together with the grand temple.

WONDERING AT THE GORGEOUSNESS

ikko structures are all beautifully planned and decorated both inside and outside. But *Daiyubyo* alone is enough to make you open your eyes wide and wonder at its gorgeousness.

Now come into the **nave.** The hanging canopy, the sutra-desks, the flower-vases, the lanterns, etc., and the decorations above and around; all glitter with gold.

The walls and the ceiling are decorated with paintings and carvings, among which the lions on the screens were painted by *Tanyu* and *Eishin Kano*, the famous artists.

The lacquer on the beams, for instance, is said to have had no less than thirty coatings, which shows how everything was done with extreme care.

NIKKO NATIONAL PARK

華麗に睹る

日光の建築物は東照宮たると大猷廟たるとを問はず、其の善美を盡した結構は事新らしく逃べるまでもないが、それ等の悉くが外觀の壯美、內陣の華麗相應ずるところ眞に名實共に美術の粹を誇るものであるが、大猷廟內陣の如き正に其の代表的のものとして眼を睜らずにはゐられない。

殿內六十三疊、中央に鍍金の天蓋を釣り、正面には金梨子地の經机を列し三具足を備へ、左右には三家より獻進にかゝる花瓶一對及和蘭獻備の玻璃燈籠一對を配し左方には樂器を陳列してゐる。天井は折揚格天井で岩群靑地に龍の置上極彩色を描き、承塵上には桐に鳳凰、羽目には牡丹唐草など何れも浮彫活彫色で、正面左右の金地大羽目に墨痕淋漓として畫かれたる獅子こそは右は探幽守信、左は永眞安信の名作である。殿の內外は悉く金の押箔を用ひ、金色燦然として絢爛目を奪ふものがある。本殿と渡殿との間、格天井には鳳凰の置上極彩色を施し、室內には加州侯より獻じた香爐燈籠等を配置してゐる。

漆塗の如きは三十回以上も塗重ね、色も黑・辯柄・朱等を混ぜ合せたもの、純朱塗、漆の上に高蒔繪・平蒔繪、梨子地彩色等、繪畫は當時の繪所預狩野探幽の監督と見られる。

華麗に睛る
Wondering at the splendour.

THE NAVE OF THE THIRD SHOGUN'S MAUSOLEUM
三代廟御内陣

THE HAIDEN (ORATORY) OF THE THIRD SHOGUN'S MAUSOLEM
三代廟拝殿

INTO THE MAUSOLEUM

Koka-mon, at the entrance to the inner temple of *Daiyubyo*, is as pretty as a picture, under the shade of thick foliage. The gate was constructed in *Ryugu-zukuri* according to the style of Ming Dynasty in China; its beautiful colours, blue, white and crimson, mingling with the green leaves of old pine-trees and cryptomerias, give the effect of magnificence beyond the human world. The name *Koka*, like *Yomei-mon*, was granted by the court. It is quite an elaborate structure. On the ceiling angels are painted.

Yasha-mon, "the Demon Gate," is the third gate of *Daiyubyo*, in the same style with *Niten-mon*; the whole gate is gilded with gold-leaves so that, shining brilliantly, it is very beautiful. Four images of demons are set in the wings of the gate; hence the name. But it is also called "the Peony Gate," because it is decorated with many pictures and carvings of tree-peonies.

Passing the gate, you will find 22 standing lanterns, two bronze ones among which were dedicated from Korea some 200 years ago.

Within a stone-fence with a bronze gate in front, stands **a sacred pagoda,** just like that of *Toshogu*, about 10 feet high, in which the soul of *Iyemitsu*, the third Shogun, sleeps forever.

NIKKO NATIONAL PARK

廟内深く

三代廟奥の院の入口にある皇嘉門は翠滴る樹々の蔭に恰も畫に見るやうな構へ――明朝の式に則つた龍宮造りで、彩粉の丹・青・白は色とりどゝに老杉・松柏に映發し、眞に人間世界を超越した莊嚴さである。皇嘉門の名は陽明門と同じく朝廷から賜つたもので、屋根は銅瓦、樓腹は蠟色、下地に白堊を塗り、内外桁は堆朱塗の地紋彫に三所葵の紋を散らし、組物は二手先詰組で極彩色を施し、地彫胡粉摺の丸桁を支へ、紅白の配合美はしく、天井に天人を描いてゐる。

夜叉門は三代廟の第三門――、建築樣式は仁天門と大差ないが、全門悉く金箔を押し光輝燦然として殊の外美觀を呈してゐる。兩面左右に四夜叉を安置してゐるのでまた夜叉門の稱があるが、牡丹の彫刻装飾が多いので牡丹門とも呼ばれ、唐門と共に壯麗の極致である。門を入れば左右に二十二基の燈籠が並列してゐるが、内二基は明暦元年朝鮮より献進した青銅製で異彩を放つてゐる。

御寶塔は高さ一丈餘、東照宮奥の院のものと同樣で、三代將軍家光公の靈を祀り、背後に石垣を築き正面に唐銅の鑄拔門を設けてゐる。

THE SACRED PAGODA AT THE INNER SHRINE,
THE THIRD SHOGUN'S MAUSOLEUM
三代廟の奥院御寶塔

廟内深く
Into the sacred bounds.

THE YASHAMON (DEMON GATE) OF
THE THIRD SHOGUN'S MAUSOLEUM
三代廟夜叉門

THE KOKAMON OF THE
THIRD SHOGUN'S MAUSOLEUM
三代廟皇嘉門

NEVER TIRED

The visit to Nikko is now favoured with speed. Take a bus, and you can go anywhere you like with speed and pleasure.

If you look from *Kanaya* Hotel, you will see the River *Daiya* shining white along the mountain foot, the mountain range towering behind in the morning haze, and the drive-way stretching long between the clear stream and the row of old cryptomerias. Just stop your car near the Sacred Bridge, and look back; beyond the pretty bridge, near the river, tower Mts. *Ogura* and *Toyama*, then *Akanagi* to their north, and then *Nyobo* and *Nakimushi* far in the distance.

The folk dance of the Nikko Copper Refining Co. is another attraction of Nikko. It is full of interests for you to see them, men and women, dance a primitive local dance, in the same attire of *yukatas* and handkerchiefs on heads, to the accompaniment of a rural band, throughout the cool breezy summer nights.

You will thus never be tired of Nikko, with the variety of natural beauty combined with arts and life which have been cultivated for the past three hundred years.

NIKKO NATIONAL PARK

訪ね行けば

今の日光見物はスピード地代に惠まれる。參道はバスに乘つて……快適な速度で飛ばし……そして訪ね行く先々の面白さ愉快さ――。

金谷ホテルから望めば山麓の彼方に帶一筋、大谷川の清流が白く光る。遙かに聳ゆる群峰は朝霧に模糊たり。大谷川に沿ふ坦々たるドライブ・ウェイは老杉と清流に挾まれて長々と續く。

神橋のほとり、暫し車を停めてかへり見すれば、神々しい丹塗の色鮮やかな橋を中心に、川對ひはすぐ小倉山・外山・その北に聳え立つ赤薙山、さては女貌山の遠望、鳴蟲山の茂みなど轉た遊子の旅情を唆る。

日光精銅所の和樂踊は町の一名物、涼風に惠まれる夏の夜を揃ひの浴衣に頬冠り、野趣たつぷりな音頭囃子につれて踊り出す、手振り足拍子の面白さ、觀光客の旅情を慰める郷土色豐かな藝術である。

THE DAIYA RIVER SEEN FROM KANAYA HOTEL
金谷ホテルより見たる大谷川

THE WAY ALONG THE DAIYA RIVER
大谷川に沿ふ街道

THE FOLK-DANCE AT THE COPPER-REFINERY, NIKKO
日光精銅所和樂踊

THE BUS RUNNING NEAR THE SACRED BRIDGE
神橋附近を走る日光バス

訪ね行けば
Still going.

UP LIKE A WIND

At *Umagaeshi*, "Horse-Turning," (because a horse cannot go up from there) you can now avail yourself of **a cable car**, and after eight minutes' ride-up like a wind, you will reach **Akechidaira**. Here you can have a great view of panorama and appreciate the greatness of god's intent; the green slope of *Tansei* Mountain-side, *Byobuiwa*, "the precipice like a paper screen," *Hoto* and *Hannya* Falls, all fusing into a pretty work of God's art. And in winter the snow-crowned Mt. *Nantai* will welcome you with its noble smile as soon as you come up here. You can never overpraise the view here. It is indeed the symphony of nature and civilization. Yet this is not all. Still another treat waits for you to come.

NIKKO NATIONAL PARK

風の如く登る

明智平とは馬返しを基點とする日光登山ケーブルによつて登り詰めたところをいふ。

この大景觀は近代交通機關たる壯快なケーブルカーとロープウエイによつて展望自在、羽化登仙の快味を滿喫することができる。丹勢山の斜面が神の匠意になつた庭園そのまゝであるに、其上、屏風岩と般若、方等の二瀑を脚下に俯瞰するところがケーブルの終點であり、驛の點景としては豪快無比、まことに天下一品と高言するに憚らぬ。

馬返しからケーブルカーで八分、その先は專用自動車で平坦な路を二、三粁、交通安全を意圖して特別の時間割により往路復路を限定運轉を行つてゐるので事故の如きは全く皆無といつてもよい。沿道はいづくも春秋ともに八汐、紅葉などの眺めあでやかに風光絕美、日光群峰中有數の景觀である。驛を出て廣場のすぐ正面から丘陵を上ると數百段にして小さい平地こそは明智平の最高峰だ。

ケーブルカー・自動車・架空索道と近代文明の所産になる交通機關は大自然の一角を征服して文化の觸手の及ぶところ、自然と文明との快適なる交響樂であり、終點驛より雪の男體山を展望した景觀のごとき、その雄大にして明澄なる眞に近代景觀の最高峰ではある。

THE MAGNIFICENT VIEW OF WATER AND MOUNTAIN

A thrill awaits you. Behold a rope way from *Akechidaira* to a still higher terrace above, **Tembodai,** "the Overlooking Terrace." If you are too timid to avail the three minutes' ride in the air line car, you can go up by bus or on foot.

Here you can fully appreciate the glory and pleasure of having conquered height. The preponderant sublimity and smartness of Mt. *Nantai*, the dark forests at its sides, the mysterious lake at its foot, the waterfalls that come from the lake, and the valleys; all these fuse into a great panorama of beauties. But look ahead, and you will see in the distance the *Nasu* Plain, the mountain ranges of *Tsukuba*, and the River *Kinu* shining silvery and winding over the plain till it disappears into the hazy horizon. Now turn your head and look towards the lake. There mountain after mountain towers and the lake lies as quiet as death among them. I am sure you will forget yourself and everything here.

NIKKO NATIONAL PARK

見晴かす山水美

大空をするゞと壯快なロープウェイに運ばれて僅か三分で展望臺に達する。

男體山の崇嚴で、重厚で、スツキリとした明るさと、それを粧ふ森の茂みと、山裾を涵す中禪寺湖の神秘さと、湖水の溢れが瀑と墜つる溪谷のゆるぎと、視野に映る眺めはパノラマ式景觀を雙眸に收めて飽くことを知らない。

大谷川の淸流が斷崖の下に東する彼方、すぐ鼻の先に男體山が放射線上の空谷を幾つも溪へおとしたまゝ悠然と聳え立つ、その山裾から腰の周りを、自動車がさながら蟻の這ふやうに上りつ下りつする、男體の右寄りを少し遠退く女貌山、東へ逸れて遙かに那須・筑波の山々、遠く鬼怒川の帶一筋、白く光つて夢のやうに野の彼方に消える。

眸を回らせば、西に開ける中禪寺湖の奧が、藍を湛へて霞に消え、水に臨む此方の湖畔には旅館、ホテルの數々、名だゝる華嚴の名瀑を銀河を倒しまに、瀑の膝下は霧に煙つて見えわかず、白雲の瀧は綿の花をのまゝ白く飛んでは白雲の彼方へ。

明智平が展望臺としての價値は、山や水や野などの廣さ深さとの交渉、姿態、運動の變化から來るもので個々に分解しては無意味だ、適度の遠近からも展望し得る所にその特權がある。

見晴かす山水美
Commanding Views.

THE AIR CABLE CAR AT AKECHIDAIRA
明智平空中ケーブルカー

THE AIR CABLE CAR AT AKECHIDAIRA
明智平空中ケーブルカー

THE DISTANT VIEW OF KEGON FALL AND LAKE CHUZENJI
華厳瀧と中禅寺湖大觀

THROUGH THE VALLEY

assing the tea-house of *Fukazawa* and *Nyonindo* and still going up the valley, you will come to the tea-house of *Kengamine*, from where you can have a distant view of two waterfalls, **Hoto-no-taki** on your right and **Hannya-no-taki** on your left, beyond the deep valley. These names, together with *Kegon* and *Agon*, are all taken from the Buddhist Scriptures according to their size.

Leaving the falls behind and still going up, we presently come to *Naka-no-chaya*. Here we can have a glance of the **Agon** cascade on the opposite mountain side.

A beautiful drive-way winds up the mountain side among the ever-greens and tinted leaves in autumn, giving you, here and there, a panoramic sight of distant views. **Godan-gaeshi,** "the Five Turnings," on the way, is rather famous for its looping way.

NIKKO NATIONAL PARK

谿を辿りて

深澤の茶屋を過ぎ、女人堂の側を經て登れば、一歩は一歩よりも高く谿を辿つて行くほどに間もなく劍ケ峰の茶屋に着く、深谷を距てゝ北を望めば二瀑あり、右の小なるを**方等**と呼び、左の大なるを**盤若**と呼ぶ、方等はその高さ五六丈、幅約一間、瀑背を潜行することが出來るので、一名小裏見の稱がある。盤若は高さ七八丈、幅二三間、水勢いと盛にして能く瀑側に近づくことが出來ない。

そも／＼方等盤若の瀑名は華嚴阿含等も同じく主としてその大きさに從ひ佛典によつて名附けられたもので、霧降、裏見の如く形狀によつて命名されたものではない。俗に往々右の小なるものを盤若とし、左の大なるものを方等と呼ぶのは甚しく誤つたものである。劍ケ峰を登れば半途に中の茶屋があり、此處より大谷の上流を距てゝ對岸の山腹に一小瀑の懸かるのを見る、是れ即ち阿含瀑でその下流は大谷川に注いでゐる。

國道八號線名所五段返しのあたり、山腹を這ふて蜒迂餘曲折する道路は林間を通じ、樹容の趣を改め、幽寂の氣身に迫るのを覺える。この堂々たるドライブウエイは幾多の大景觀を縫ふてバスにタクシーに近代交通の觸手めでたく、國道改修の整然たるところを見せてゐる。

[23]

HAN-NYA FALL
磐若の瀧

HOTO FALL
方等の瀧

谿を辿りて
Through the valley.

THE FIVE-TURNINGS ON THE CHUZENJI-WAY.
中禪寺道五段返し

ROARING WITH THE SACRED RHYTHM

A mighty cataract hangs,
    With water rushing voluminously down,
Dashing a thousand yards, nay,
    Ten thousand yards in a jump.

So sung by *Kozan Ono*, an ancient poet, **Kegon-no-taki** is the most widely known throughout the country. It is an overflow of the lake-water and thunders down more than 330 feet with the everlasting sacred rhythm. It makes one of the trio of the natural beauty of Nikko, the other two being Mt. *Nantai* and Lake *Chuzenji*.

It looks from a distance just like a white silk hanging from the precipice, but once you go near, it blows wind and gale and raises a cloud of sprays all around the basin.

Geologists say that the eruption of Mt. *Nantai* dammed up the River *Daiya* into Lake *Chuzenji*, whose overflow falls as *Kegon* from the high cliff, while undercurrents going under the earth, gush out again as the Nikko twelve cascades.

The basin of *Kegon* is 7 and 10 yards wide each, and is always covered with the white mist, so that you cannot look into it. It can now be reached by an elevator from the tea-house above.

NIKKO NATIONAL PARK

神韻を籠めて

水勢奔飛大瀑懸、一落千丈又萬丈、小野湖山の吟じた天下の巨瀑華嚴は日光の自然景觀中、山の男體、水の中禪寺湖に併せてトリオを奏づるもの、まことにその名は重く、深く、強く、限りなき神韻を籠めて轟きわたる。

瀑の高きこと、正に三百六十尺、との直下三十六丈が、まるで素練をかけたやうに、絶壁をそゝぎ墜つる威容の神々しさ、その奔流と亂舞が、霧をおこし、風を呼び、飛沫を散らして夏なほ肌寒い感じがする。華嚴の瀧は男體山の噴出によつて生じたもので、粗なる集塊岩は元の地盤をなす石英斑岩の堆上に積まれ、更に熔岩の厚層をもつて蔽はれ、大谷の溪流を堰止めて中禪寺湖を生成したもので、湖面の水は華嚴の瀧となつて落下し、湖底の水は地下を潜行して十二瀑となり、今日の大景觀を造つたものである。瀑壺は廣さ三十間、長さ二十間にあまり、常に水沫濛々として白煙のごとく、よく瀑底を覘ひ知ることができない。もと、此名瀑は正面から雄姿を見ることが出來なかつたのを中宮祠の人、星野五郎平翁が之を遺憾とし六十の高齡を以て千辛萬苦、遂に明治卅三年十月に現今の新路を開き、正面に瀧を仰いで名瀑の眞面目を發揮せしめたものである。近頃はエレヴエーターにて瀧壺に到る事も出來る樣になつた。

INTERESTING WITH DIFFERENT ASPECTS

If you want to know perfectly the beauty of this famous waterfall, **Kegon**, you must look at it from every angle.

First look it up from the *Gorobei-jaya*, a tea-house, near the basin; next look it down from the *Kegon-jaya*, or from *Takimi-dai*, "the fall viewing terrace," a little below the tea-house; and then from *Akechidaira* afar. It gives you a different aspect and feeling every time. But the most mysterious and wonderful is the aspect of the falls frozen into crystal icicles. Then Nature stops its eternal rhythm of thunder, and a deep silence reigns over the death of this mighty king.

Kegon! Kegon! It is indeed the king of waterfalls in the whole country.

Near the *Kegon* Fall, with a projecting cliff between them, is **Shirakumo-no-taki,** "the White Cloud Cascade," an entirely different aspect from the *Kegon*, though so near.

It is the fall of gushing water from the undercurrent among the crags, while the Kegon is an overflow from the lake. Though its water is quite abundant, it has a rather female aspect compared with the mightiness of its masculine neighbour. You can have its best view from a bridge, *Kasasagi-bashi*, across it.

NIKKO NATIONAL PARK

興趣限りなく

華嚴の瀧は、瀑壺に降りて五郎平茶屋附近から仰ぎ見るのと、華嚴茶屋、若くは稍下つた中腹の瀑見臺から下向ひに見るのと、明智平から遙かに瞰下するのと、三位三態の趣があり、興趣さまぐゝで限りがない。天下の華嚴を完全に認識しやうとするにはあらゆる視角から、再吟味三檢討の必要があり、五郎平茶屋の壯觀、瀑見臺の奇觀、明智平の遠望、いづれ劣らぬ瀑の生命は脈々として盡きない。見上げ見下す峽間を縱橫に、幾萬とも知らぬ岩雀の群が翔け上り舞ひ下る。天から墜ちる瀑布が雷と鳴り、飛沫の霧が秋を霑ほす豪宕と淸麗の二重奏は瀑布國の日本でも遙かに群小瀑布を壓してその王座に君臨してゐる。

華嚴の瀑に對して不卽不離の關係にある**白雲の瀧**は斷崖の一突角を隔てゝ華嚴と相隣るのであるが、姿態も氣分もこの二つは全く異つた感じで、華嚴が湖面からの溢れ水であるのに反し、白雲は斷崖の中途から迸り出づる地下滲透水であり、且つ急斜面を流下するととてその雄渾さでは多少見劣りはするが、水量は豐富で高さも三十丈・中腹に架つてゐる鵲橋(カササギバシ)からの展望など、飽くまでも雄大なる華嚴に較べて、殊に結氷期の物凄いほどの偉觀に比して、これはまた飽くまでも瀟洒たる小品の感じである。

WAFERFALLS

hat contributes much to making Nikko the park of the world is its water views, especially those of its many waterfalls.

Kirifuri-no-taki, "the Mist Falling Cascade," about four miles from the Sacred Bridge, can be reached by passing the *Ritsuin* and *Umeyashiki* and going northward round the foot of Mt. *Ogura*. It is one of the three most famous falls in Nikko, and is considered the most picturesque. The water falls about 300 feet, stepping twice on the way and thus scattering the mist all around; hence the name.

Urami-no-taki, "the Back Viewing Cascade," also one of the three, stands about a mile from *Urami* Station. As the name indicates, it can be seen from behind, because the brittle rock under the head of the fall has been worn away and men can go behind the water.

Gamman-ga-fuchi is a deep abyss in the River *Daiya* amid a jumble of fantastic rocks, about a mile up from the Sacred Bridge. On the face of a big rock are inscribed the sanscrit characters "Gamman." And near the abyss stand a row of Buddhist stone-images, *Gohyaku-Rakan*.

NIKKO NATIONAL PARK

瀑布に見る

溪谷のせまるところ、墜ちては千丈の飛瀑となる、世界の公園日光をして錦上更に花を添へるものに、惠まれたる幾多の名瀑がある。

霧降の瀧は神橋から東北約一里半、板穴川の上流にあり、稲荷川を渡り律院、梅屋敷を經、小倉山の東南部を廻り北行すれば暫時にして望瀑臺に達する。その北方眼前に恰かも白布を懸けたやうなのが日光三名瀑の一つである霧降の瀧で、高さ約三百尺、一の瀧二の瀧の二段をなし、水流二派にわかれて巖壁を奔り恰も玉簾を懸けたごとく飛沫は煙霧と散つて眞に霧降の名に背かない。

裏見の瀧は同じく日光三名瀑の一つとして荒澤の瀑とも稱へ裏見停車場の西北十數丁の地にあり、高さ五六丈、幅約六尺、飛沫は雨のごとく降つて四周を潤す。瀑は集塊岩を蔽ひ突出する熔岩上より奔下するものであつて、崩壞した集塊岩を削り小徑を通じ、かくして背後より見ることが出來るので此名がある。

含滿ケ淵は大谷川の激流が茲に奇岩怪石の爲に阻められて青淵を作り、その深さは測りがたく凄壯を極め、巨巖疊々として水涯より峙ち、その奇はたゞ鬼工といふの外はない。又巨岩の面にはカンマンの大梵字が刻まれてゐる。

瀧布に見る
The Wonder Falls

KIRIFURI FALL
霧降瀧

URAMI FALL
裏見の瀧

GAMMAN ABYSS
含満ヶ淵

URAMI FALL
裏見の瀧

A CALM MORNING

The radiant sunshine salutes the tops of Nikko mountains and the quiet morning smiles upon the beautiful forest of white birches.

In the early morning, you may trace the winding way up the valley along the River *Daiya*, breathing a fresh air, now listening to the chattering brook, now wondering at the fanciful rocks, and now hurrying away from the dashful torrents, until at last you will come to **Odaira,** an even space. There the slender, white birches with their silvery skin among the shrubs will at once catch your eyes. And when you are dreaming a dream with your hand on the white skin, you will perhaps be awakened by the shrilling cries of birds, and sometimes of monkeys.

But still go on along the lane, and soon you will come to the *Kegon* Elevator Station and *Chugushi* Station of the Nikko Mountaineering Railway. Here your dream or meditation in the calm morning will be put an end to by the modern civilization.

NIKKO NATIONAL PARK

靜かなる朝

すがすがしい朝の太陽は白樺林の上に美しく光り輝き、靜かなる朝は日光群峰をめぐつて展け行く、馬返から中禪寺湖畔の大平までは羊腸の險路、一氣に登れば大平へと着く。

山内から大平までは常に大谷川峽谷を溯るのだが、この間、溪谷の幽邃と、水勢の變幻と、斷崖の奇峭が連繞數里に亘る景觀美は他に匹儔を見ない。それは日光火山群の山といふ山から絞り出す水が永い間の侵蝕作用を續けた揚句、すべて此の川一筋にあつまつて流れるからである。登り果てたといふ氣安さと共に、熊笹の生えた廣場が急に展けて、落葉松・ミヅナラ・などの高山植林や矮草灌木の繁生する中に、銀の柱ともまがふ白樺の群落が、清らけくも美しく、落ついた旅人の心を捉へる。杖を停めて朝の大氣にうるんだ樹皮の和肌を撫でても見よう、滑らかな感觸が指先へ滲みこんでは詩の心、歌の姿が遊子の胸に感傷をたゝへる。まことに偉大なる靜けさ、この靜けさの中を時折奏でる鳥の聲と岩猿の叫びとに夢を破られる。

登り詰めた大平から白樺の木立を行くと、やがて人家も疎らに、華嚴觀瀑エレヴェーター、日光登山鐵道の中宮祠驛、各自動車の停留所、モーター會社等があり夢は現實へとかへる。

THE GROVE OF WHITE BIRCHES
IN THE MORNING MIST
朝霧かゝる大平の白樺林

靜かなる朝
The quiet morning.

THE GROVE OF WHITE BIRCHES
IN THE MORNING MIST
朝霧かゝる大平の白樺林

LAKE CHUZENJI

ake *Chugushi* is popularly called **Chuzenji-ko** and sometimes *Nanko*, "South Lake." It was also granted the name *Sachino-umi*, "The Happy Lake," by the Emperor *Meiji*, when His Majesty paid a visit here.

The lake, about 8 and 2 miles wide each, is the source of the natural beauty of Nikko; the rivers and waterfalls all come out of this lake. But the lake itself stands highest in beauty among these beauty spots of Nikko.

The beautiful face like a mirror, the pure and abundant water, the rich foliage of the trees on the beach, and the majestic mountains surrounding it; all these go to make it the queen of Nikko beauties.

And once you get into a boat or a yacht, why, you will feel you are in a fairyland. In spring a hazy mist will cover up the dreamy lake; in summer a cool breeze will kiss the white surges in the lingering twilight; in autumn the moon will shine over the silver ripples; and in winter a death-like calmness will reign over the snow-bound surroundings. You can enjoy its beauty throughout all seasons.

NIKKO NATIONAL PARK

湖上を航る

中禪寺湖は中宮祠湖又は南湖とも稱へ、明治天皇陛下御巡幸の砌、名を幸湖（サチノウミ）と賜つた。東西三里弱、南北約一里、周圍七里餘、湖水清澄にして眞砂を數ふべく、洋々たる湖面に一の漂芥を見るなく、翠山四方を環り、樹木鬱蒼として影を鏡面に浸し、神意あくまでも清く、雲煙の集散するところ、晴によく雨に奇、若し夫れ扁舟に棹さゝんか、身は仙境にあつて山水美の極致に恍惚の情を禁じ得ない。赤、駘蕩の春、煙霞模糊たるの時、湖心は春風に和いで夢の如く、夏日薄暮、涼風湖面を吹いて萬斛の涼味掬すゐにあまりあり、仲秋、月に臨んでは一幅、水墨の畫景そのまゝ、更に滿目蕭條たる雪の湖景こそは正に清寂境の醍醐味を滿喫させる。蓋し湖水の四季、その感興の盡くるところを知らない。

舟を湖心に泛べて男體山を仰ぐ時、巨人と聳え立つ山容の雄姿、鏡のごとき水態の靜寂、山神・水神相呼應して知らず〲、神秘の夢幻境に誘ふ、まことや、中禪寺湖こそは、まさに神の造りませし壯嚴端麗の景觀美、以て世界に誇るべきもの、太古の如き大いなる靜寂に加へて、近代湖沼美の精粹また竟めて此處にあり、建築物の美觀壯觀、山岳美の雄大無比に併せて、惠まれたるかな、大景觀日光よ。

湖上を航る
Yachting on the lake.

SAILING ON LAKE CHUZENJI
中禅寺湖上のセーリング

THE BRIDGE AT THE LAKE-TAIL

High mountains behind mountains enclose a lake; they reflect themselves on the mirror of the lake in their different attire according to the season. And the water is as blue and deep as possible; how shall I express the sense of that deep quietness which seems to penetrate into our heart.

As soon as the boat leaves the beach, you will notice that the water becomes suddenly deep like a pail, and the fish are swimming in every direction in the clear water. A little deeper, and the big rocks look like oxen squatting at the bottom and the sunken trunks like water-snakes crawling, as the waves sway. But soon the bottom darkens. Look up! The majestic Mt. *Nantai* is nearer to you and smiles upon you.

Now look at the place where the lake narrows into a river. It is called *Ojiri*, and the bridge over it is called the **Ojiri Bridge**.

The festival of visiting the inner shrine of Mt. *Nantai* is held every year for a week from August 1. As soon as the clock strikes twelve at midnight, thousands of visitors, all in white and with Kongo-sticks and lanterns, rush out of the climbing gate of the *Chugushi-shrine* up into the depths of the forest, till they get to the top, where they wait to see the sun rise in the east. The plate shows these visitors waiting for the time, near the lake.

NIKKO NATIONAL PARK

湖尻に架る

高い山が重なり合つて湖を圍んでゐる。しかも其の山々は四季折々に粧ひを更めて水鏡に姿を映す。水は飽くまで碧く深く、その落ちついた、人の肌に滲み透るやうな寂寞の氣分を何に譬へよう。

舟が岸を離れたかと思ふと、水は急に桶の底のやうに深くなる、清澄な水底を、魚族が縱横に群り泳ぐ、五米、十米と深まりゆけば、湖底の巖は牛の蹲るがごとく、幾抱へもある程の沈んだ大木が波にゆらるてうねくねと這ふ不氣味さ、やがてそれも見え分かぬほどに水底が暗くなる。眼は水から岸へ、岸から山へと移り行く。

湖水の流れ出るところを大尻と呼び、こゝに架した橋を大尻橋といふ。

男體山の奧宮登拜祭は毎年八月一日から七日まで行はれ、深更十二時を合圖に幾千の登拜團は、いづれも白衣の裝束で、金剛杖をつき、提灯を手にし、中宮祠登拜門から雪崩を打つて、森の奧へ〳〵と驅け登り、山頂を究めて莊嚴無比の御來迎を拜するのであるが、年々の登拜者は非常の多數に上る。圖は登拜者が中禪寺湖畔に屯して時を待つ光景である。

湖尻に架る
The bridge over the lake tail.

THE BEACH OF LAKE CHUZENJI
NEAR THE FUTARA SHRINE
中禪寺湖畔 二荒神社下

THE OJIRI BRIDGE
大尻橋

THE CROWD AT THE CLIMBING
FESTIVAL OF MT. NANTAI
男体山登拜祭の賑ひ

THE OJIRI BRIDGE AT
THE LAKE-TAIL
中禪寺湖口の大尻橋

KANNON-DO

If you go along the *Utagahama* Beach, you will get to **Tachiki Kannon**, after passing a few hotels and the pretty villas of foreign embassies and legations here and there among the trees, which give an exotic effect upon the scene.

There is a legend about *Tachiki Kannon* that when *Dosho*, the virtuous priest, was saying a mass there, an angel came down from heaven and sang an anthem to it. The temple was built only in 1913, in the style of *hokei-zukuri*, with a roof of copper tiles. *Kannon*, the principal image of the temple, has a tradition of its own. *Dosho-shonin*, the virtuous, tried to climb Mt. *Nantai* twice but in vain, then he carved an image of the thousand-handed *Kannon* on a big tree growing there and prayed, and he could accomplish his will, conquering the mountain. The image is about 16 feet high and is now set in the temple with other images attributed to *Unkei*, an ancient famous engraver. There are also other accessory structures there. The scenery here is one of the best in Nikko, with the lake and the beautiful surroundings; the white sails of a boat or a yacht sometimes skip over the shadows of the pretty *torii* and Mt. *Nantai* reflecting on the lake face. And in summer, it becomes an ideal camping place, worthy of the name of a utopia or a fairyland.

NIKKO NATIONAL PARK

観音堂に詣でゝは

大尻橋より渚傳ひに行くと一、二旅館と歌ケ濱立木観音があり、外に木立の間に外國大公使館、其他の別荘が建ち並び、どことなく國際的な異國風景だ、立木観音堂は勝道上人修法の際、天人天降つて詠歌讃嘆せられたといふ由緒があり、寳形造六間四面銅葺で大正二年十月竣工、坂東十八番の札所であるが、本尊は――勝道上人が男體の頂上を極めんとし、兩回迄志を果すことができなかつたので、立木に千手観音を刻んで祈念し、終に目的を達したといふ――その因縁深い尊像で、高さ一丈六尺、左右には雲慶作といふ四天王を安置し、附近には鐘樓・吉祥堂・金剛堂などがある。

此のあたり、湖面のすが〳〵しさと四邊景觀の絶佳は湖畔風景の白眉で、靜かな湖面に倒影する男體山の雄姿、汀に立つ玲瓏たる華表――そしてこゝ彼處に浮ぶ小舟も一入の風情を添へて、無くてはならぬ點景である。

青嵐、涼風清々しい夏ともなれば絶好のキャンプ地として此世からなるユートピアを現出し、眞に仙境の名にふさはしいものがある。

観音堂に詣では
The Kannondo.

UTAGAHAMA BEACH, LAKE CHUZENJI
中禅寺歌ヶ濱

TACHIKI-KANNON, CHUZENJI
中禅寺 立木観音

BOATING ON THE LAKE

he *Chugushi* Shrine stands where Mt. *Futara* and Lake *Chuzenji* come nearest. Making it a starting point, beautiful roads run, one to the west as far as **Shobu-ga-hama** Beach and the other to the south as far as *Tanuki-kubo*. *Chugushi* is a one-sided street, with houses and hotels facing the lake, and commanding a fine view of *Utagahama* Beach, *Tozawa*, *Hatcho-Deshima*, *Kozuke-jima* and *Teragasaki*.

If you get on a motor boat at the **pier** and come out on the lake, what a pleasure you can have! Far in the distance nobly tower Mts. *Shirane* and *Onsen* with the white snow on their peaks even in June, and near along the beach lies the tunnel of flowers in spring and of maple leaves in autumn. And pretty villas spot the scene.

Teragasaki is a long promontory projecting far into the lake, with *Yakushido* at the tip.

Kozukejima is a tiny isle, with a tower in the centre in which is treasured the bones of *Dosho-shonin*, the virtuous priest.

Shiraiwa is a heap of white rocks on the west beach.

NIKKO NATIONAL PARK

THE PIER FOR BOATS, LAKE CHUZENJI
中禪寺湖ボート發着所

船を泛べて
The boating pleasures.

TERAGASAKI, LAKE CHUZENJI
中禪寺湖 寺ヶ崎

NEAR AKAIWA, LAKE CHUZENJI
中禪寺湖 赤岩附近

SHOBU-GA-HAMA BEACH, LAKE CHUZENJI
中禪寺湖畔 菖蒲ヶ濱

THE NEIGHBOURHOOD OF SHIRAIWA, LAKE CHUZENJI
中禪寺湖 白岩附近

KOZUKE ISLE, LAKE CHUZENJI
中禪寺湖 上野島

BOATS ON LAKE CHUZENJI
中禪寺湖々上のボート

THE RAPIDS

ow let us leave the lake behind and take our course to *Yumoto*; just a stretch of road with woods on the right and a beach on the left. The more you go, the more white birches will salute you. Then comes **Ryuzu-no-taki,** "the Dragons' Heads Falls." It might as well be called a torrent. The water runs down for about a quarter mile on the rugged river bed so rapidly that it looks like the heads of dragons racing up the river. The magic of water increases as you go along the river until at last you will arrive at the head of *Senjo-ga-hara*, "The Battle Field Plain."

If you turn to the right there and go along a lane for a fifth mile, you will come to a deep cave called **Jigoku-no-kama,** "The Hell Cave." This is the source of the *Jigoku-gawa*, "The Hades." But let us go back to the main road, and make our way until we come to the tea-house of **Akanuma,** "The Red Marsh." *Akanuma* is now nothing but a swamp, but it was once a big lake and let out its water to the Hell Cave, according to the opinion of geologists.

NIKKO NATIONAL PARK

RYUTO FALL, NIKKO
日光 龍頭の瀧

岩角に激しつゝ
The rapids

FULL OF POETRY

he summer grass all over the field,
　　Where warriors fought and died,
　　　The land of their empty dreams!
　　　　　　(A *Haiku* by *Basho*)

　The name of **Senjo-ga-hara**, "The Battle Field Dlain," is indeed full of poetic and past-recalling sentiments. Some say that it was a battle field fought by ancient gods, and others say that *Naotaka Oda*, Lord of *Hitachi*, when he rebelled against the *Kamakura* Shogunate, fought with the punitive force here. But the present view of *Senjo-ga-hara* far surpasses the historical beauty.

　Most of the plain is a swamp dotted here and there with lumps of larch-trees, but in June it turns into a tremendous flower bed, all the plants blooming with omnifarious colours at the same time.

　There are three pine trees in the centre of the plain. Near the tea-house, the way divides itself into two, the right one leading to the *Nishizawa* Gold Mine and the left one to the *Yumoto* Hot Springs.

　This table land was once a lake, even larger than Lake *Chuzenji*, but was reclaimed by the erruptions of Mts. *Nantai* and *Shirané*; ; the present plain of four kilometres on each side is nothing but the remnants of the volcanic actions.

　If you turn to the left from the main road, you will hear the sounds of a waterfall, **Yutaki** by name, about 450 feet high. Though a very beautiful fall, it is known to a very few people, on account of the inconvenience of communication.

NIKKO NATIONAL PARK

詩情溢るゝ

　夏草やつはものどもの夢の跡……まことに戰場ケ原の名は懷古的情趣ゆたかに、詩情が溢れてゐる。此處は上古神戰の跡、又は嘉慶年間、常陸の小田入道直高が鎌倉殿に叛いて討伐軍と戰つた遺跡とも傳へられ、其起因はいづれとも定め難いが、戰場ケ原の景觀の美はそんな史實を超越してゐる。

　原の大部分は濕地で唯、落葉松が所々に點在してゐるばかり、六月頃になつて始めて百花一時に咲き、姸を競ふのでこれをお花畑と稱へる。原の中央に三本松あり、茶屋のあたりで道は岐れ、右すれば西澤金山に至り、左すれば湯本溫泉に達する。

　此地一帶はもと〲今の中禪寺湖よりも大きな湖水であつたのを男體、白根兩火山噴出當時に埋立られたもので、今日の南北四粁餘、東西四粁の廣漠たる原は火山活動の遺跡なのである。

　本道と分れ左へ入ること三四丁にして**湯瀧**の瀑壑を耳にする。高さ四十五丈、幅十五六間の大瀑布で水は急峻な巖壁の斜面を奔下して雄壯を極め、三名瀑にも比肩すべきものである。

・・日光國立公園・・

A SPA ON THE LAKE-SIDE

Lake Yunoko, with a dimension of a mile and a quarter from north to south and less than a mile from east to west, is surrounded with the rich foliage of old trees and is a fairyland with its fine views and sequestered calmness. A narrow promontory called *Usagi-shima* projects into the lake, which abounds with carps and other fishes. In the calm summer evenings, the cool refreshing breeze skips over the mysterious lake-face leaving ripples behind, which die away very soon. But the snow view in winter is beyond description. The mirror-like lake, which reflected the snow-capped mountains, freezes without a sound in the evening twilight, while the mists and steams of hot water that springs near the lake drift faintly and soon die over the ice-bound lake.

Walking along the beach to the north, you will soon get to the **Yumoto Spa**. It is also called the *Chugushi* Spa, a little village of about twenty houses, most of which are hotels. Each hotel has its own baths, but there are many common baths in the village. The water is of sulphur and of various temperatures, and is said to have a wonderful efficacy for the diseases of stomach, intestine, skin, eyes and women. It is well-known as an ideal summer resort.

NIKKO NATIONAL PARK

湖畔に湧く

湯の湖は南北凡そ十七八町、東西十二三丁、四邊は翠綠まさに滴らんとする老樹に圍まれ、幽邃閑雅、風光絕佳の仙境である。東北方の小牛島を兎島といひ、湖中には鯉や鮒の川魚が多く、旅客の食膳を賑はせてゐる。

靜かな夏の夕など、湖面は千古の謎をたゝへて神秘そのもののごとく、嵐氣を含んだ涼風が身に沁みる。殊に冬の雪景は何ものにもたとへやうない寂かさで、白皚々の山々を映す湖面は音もなく結氷し、ほのかなる溫泉の煙にたよふ閑寂の趣は形容の詞さへないほどである。

坦々たる湖岸の道を辿り湖の北端に達すると此處は湯元溫泉である。

湯元は一に中宮祠溫泉ともいひ戸數二十餘あり、大部分は溫泉旅館で、旅館にはいづれも內湯の設備があるが、その外に河原の湯・中の湯・御所の湯・姥の湯・笹の湯・自在湯・荒湯・蓼の湯・鶴の湯等の共同浴場がある。泉質はいづれも硫黄泉で、溫度は高低種々あり、胃腸病・皮膚病・眼病・婦人病其他に奇蹟的な特效があり、土地高燥にして飽くまでも靜寂、昔ながらの仙境、理想的避暑地として謳はれてゐる。

湖畔に湧く
The gushing spa near the lake.

LAKE YUNOKO AND THE SPA
湯の湖と日光温泉場

LAKE YUNOKO AND THE SPA IN WINTER
冬の湯の湖と温泉場

THE HOT-SPRING SOURCE, NIKKO SPA
日光温泉元湯

A SEQUESTERED NOOK

unoko, "the Hot-Water Lake," caused by the eruption of Mt. *Mitsudaké*, lies at the foot of Mt. *Shirané*, and is much smaller and shallower than Lake *Chuzenji*, but on account of the beautiful woods on the beach, it excells itself in the exquisite silence, sequestered from the madding crowd. A long promontory called **Usagi-shima**, "the Rabbit Isle," makes it the prettier. **Yunodaira**, on the north of the lake, was once the bottom of the lake, but now prospers as a spa with inns and hotels. Stay a while here. You can enjoy yourself, now walking by the calm, mysterious lake, now angling trouts in it, and now making excursions into the still inner parts of the Shirané Mountain range.

This place has recently become quite famous also as a good ski-ing resort in winter.

NIKKO NATIONAL PARK

幽邃に描く

湯の湖は白根山麓に位するが三つ岳の噴火による堰塞湖で、中禪寺湖とは比較にならぬほどに小さいが、栂の美しい林が鬱然として峰に迫る背景から、却つて幽邃な趣に富み、湖面は南北に長く、東側湖岸には兎島といふ撞木狀の小半島が突出し、湖北は曾て湖底に沒してゐたのが、今は湯ノ平となつて硫黃泉が湧き、溫泉宿が軒を並べてゐる。

白根の山影を映した湖面はあくまでも靜寂そのものでまるで太古の謎を秘めたやうに、神秘の色を漂はしてゐるなんともいへない明媚な風景である上に、溫泉と、湖水の鱒釣りと山の散步といふ好條件に惠まれ、遊覽休養地としての湯元は將來大いに有望であり、特に奥日光開發と共に、金精、白根から、菅沼・丸沼・さては最奧の尾瀨方面探勝につれて、湯元はその要地たるべき幸運を荷ふであらうし、旅館其他の設備も近來著しく改善されてゐる。赤沼ケ原から湯の湖畔へ來て、官能的な硫黃の香を嗅ぎながら溫泉宿へ寛いだ心地は遊び疲れた子供が母の懷へ抱かれるやうな懷しい氣持であり、一浴のほてりを湖畔の散策にさます時、遊子の胸は甘い感傷に甦る。なほ、附近は冬季、スキー場として最近特に全國的に有名となつてゐる。

ON THE MOUNTAIN TOP

t. **Shirané** consists of *Mae-Shirané* (the front summit) and *Oku-Shirané* (the inner summit). Though one of the Nikko mountains, it does not geologically belong to the Nikko Volcanic Range, now extinct in action. It made eruptions in 1873 and 1889. It was once said that Mt. *Shirané* was a double volcano. the front summit being a somma, the inner summit the central crater-hill, and Lake **Goshiki** the crater-lake. But the assumption was wrong. The two summits were caused by different eruptions, and Lake *Goshiki* was a mere dammed-up lake by the eruption of the inner summit.

Half a mile from the *Yumoto Spa* towards the *Konsei* Pass, and you will arrive at the foot of the mountain. As you go up, the sea of clouds will spread under your eyes, but on a fine day you can have a distant view of Lake *Chuzenji* and *Akanuma-ga-hara*, nothing to say of *Yunoko* and the hotels of *Yumoto*. But go on until at last you will come to the top, an even space where a tiny stone shrine called **Tarozan shrine** stands. The view from here is splendid. Lake *Goshiki* among the greens under your eyes and the towering summit of *Oku-Shirané* in your front play a duet of beauty.

NIKKO NATIONAL PARK

頂に立てば

日光群峰中の**白根山**は、前白根と奥白根から成り立つ、これは日光火山群と隣接してゐるが、系統は全く別で、日光火山群が有史前の舊噴火であるに對し、白根山は明治六年及同二十二年にも噴火してゐる。これまでの説では、前白根を外輪山、奥白根を中央火口丘と見る二重式火山で、**五色沼**は其間に出來た火口原湖であるとされてゐたが、實はさうではなく前白根は鬼怒沼・溫泉・金精の諸山へかけて一帶に噴火した第二紀末葉の噴火岩で奥白根とは別であり、隨つて五色沼は火口原湖ではなく、奥白根噴出のため、前白根兩側の谷が堰塞られたもので、菅沼・丸沼等と同成因と見るのが普通である。

湯元温泉から金精峠へ向けて數丁すると、白根山神社境内となる。登りつめると同時に美しい雲海が現はれ、晴れ間には湯元の温泉旅館・湯の湖・赤沼ヶ原・中禪寺湖までが見える。更に十數丁登ると平坦な所へ出る。そこの石造小社が白根山前宮で俗に之を**太郎山神社**と呼び、脚下には五色湖が深綠をたゝへ、すぐ對ひには奥白根の嶺が天を衝いて聳え立つ、山容の雄大と位置の深さと、それがもつ山と麓の深林の美しさなど、頂に立つて、數時間を費すのは愉快なことであらう。

頂に立てば
On the top

THE SHIRANESAN SHRINE AT THE TOP OF MT. SHIRANE
白根山頂の白根山神社

MT. OKU-SHIRANE AND MT. MAE-SHIRANE
奥白根山と前白根山

MT. OKU-SHIRANE AND MARSH GOSHIKI
奥白根山と五色沼

LOOKING TOWARDS SUGANUMA MARSH FROM MT. SHIRANE
白根山より菅沼を望む

MT. SHIRANE SEEN FROM SHIRO-TOGE
四郎峠より見た白根山の雄姿

LOOKING TOWARDS LAKE CHUZENJI FROM MT. SHIRANE
白根山より中禅寺湖を望む

FROM THE PASS

Mt. Konsei, towering to the north of Mt. *Shirané*, makes one of the three highest, together with Mt. *Onsengatake*, among the Nikko mountains. The way through the plain at the north of the lake leads you to the *Nishizawa* Gold Mine. The beauty of the high forest on the way from *Yumoto* to the *Konsei* Pass is never inferior to that of the *Chichibu* Alps; the clumps of *Kometsuga* here and there, the snake-rooted bamboos covering the earth, and *Saruogaze* (lichen), covered with silver thaw, hanging from above; all these add to the beauty.

If you go still farther along the mountain side of *Onsengatake*, you will come to the **Konsei** Shrine on the Pass, 2,000 metres above the sea-level. The view from here is wonderful. The mirror-like lake of *Yunoko*, Mt. *Nantai*, *Senjogahara* etc., all spread like a picture under your eyes. And if it is winter, the splendour of the snow-crowned landscape is quite beyond comparison.

Only, these parts are seldom visited, except by mountaineering experts or biologists, so that you will need a guide, if you want to come this way.

NIKKO NATIONAL PARK

峠を辿る

白根山に對して北に控へる**金精山**は溫泉岳とともに日光群峰の三高峰をなすもので、湖の北岸は少しの平地でこゝを通ずる一筋の道路は切込湖を經て西澤金山に至る。

湯元から**金精峠**までの深林の美しさは秩父アルプスのそれに劣らぬものがあり、そこにはコメツガの群落や、下には一面にネマガリダケが隙間もなく、土を覆ひ上からはサルヲガゼ（霧氷）の懸垂地衣が美觀を添へてゐる。湯の平から奥へ〳〵と、やがて溫泉岳中腹の赤岩を右に負笈岩を左に空谷を橫ぎつて上りつめると**金精神社**の前で、こゝが海拔二千米の峠の頂上である。そこを西へ白檜の密林を下ること八粁にして、碧水を湛へた菅沼が展ける。金精峠より湯の湖の展望は油畫のやうな構圖と配色とによつて展開され、其處に神祕の夢幻境を誘ふものがあり、同じく男體山・湯の湖・戰場ケ原等と展望の雄大にして壯美なるは、全く谿谷美の一異彩である。

たゞ、此方面は人煙殆ど絕えた交通未開の所謂日光奥地で、健脚家や動植物硏究家の爲に開かれた寶庫であるが、山の經驗乏しきものは勿論案內者を伴ふ必要があらう。

[37]

LOOKING TOWARDS LAKE
YUNOKO FROM THE PASS KONSEI
金精峠より湯の湖を望む

THE KONSEI SHRINE
金精神社

峠をたどる
The mountain climbing.

LOOKING TOWARDS LAKE YUMOTO AND
MT. NANTAI FROM THE PASS KONSEI
金精峠より湯元湖及男体山を望む

LOOKING TOWARDS THE PASS
KONSEI FROM LAKE YUNOKO
湯の湖より金精峠を望む

MIST-SNOW
霧氷

LAKES

akes and marshes play an important role in the beauty of the National Park of Nikko.

Besides Lakes *Chuzenji* and *Yunoko* which I have already mentioned, there are many lakes and marshes in Nikko; *Kirikomi-ko, Karikomi-ko, Suga-numa, Maru-numa, Kinu-numa,* etc.

If you proceed from *Yunoko* to the north round the foot of Mt. *Mitsugatake*, two lakes **Karikomi** and **Kirikomi** will welcome you. But these twin lakes connected each other with a strip of water are incomparably smaller than *Yunoko*, and in winter when they freeze into ice, groups of bears and antelopes come and go on the top of the lakes.

Lakes *Suga-numa, Maru-numa,* and *Ojiri-numa* lie in tiers. Lake **Suga-numa** is 1719 metres above the sea level and 75 metres deep at the deepest spot, though most of the lake is rather shallow. It has a very fine view, owing to the variety of the beach-line and the rich growth of trees near the water.

Maru-numa lies 30 metres lower than the former, and Hatcho-taki, "The Half Mile Falls," hangs between them.

Kinu-numa, 2,040 metres high, is a plateau marsh consisting of more than forty pools and has the plant clumps unique to the Alpine marsh. The Alpine flora in full bloom is a special attraction in summer.

NIKKO NATIONAL PARK

沼に題す

國立公園日光は建築美に、山岳美に、谿谷美に、打つて一丸とした大自然美を成してゐる中にも、殊に湖沼の姿は此大景觀の上に重要な役割を占めてゐる。中禪寺湖や湯の湖に次で是非とも紹介せねばならぬものは、切込湖・刈込湖・菅沼・丸沼・鬼怒沼などの各湖沼だ、湯の湖溫泉を出て北へ三ッ岳の腰を上ると刈込・切込の湖水巡りとなる。刈込と切込は二つの湖水らしくも見えるが、頸を締めたところの溝で聯つてゐるので湯の湖とは比較にならぬほど小さく、冬期結氷期にはカモシカや熊の群が湖面を往來する。菅沼・丸沼は大尻沼と共に段級的に層々と並んでゐるもので、最深部は七五米もあり、水際に迫る淺瀬が發達してゐるが、海拔一七一九米、多くの森林の茂みやら肢節のある湖岸線の多變化により風致が優れてをり、丸沼は低くして水準三〇米も下位にあり、其間に八丁瀧のかゝつてゐる點から見ても如何に厚層の熔岩が菅沼を堰塞めてゐるかゞ窺はれる。鬼怒沼は上下野州境に位置し、海拔二〇四〇米もある高層濕地で、東西三町、南北五町餘、大小四十有餘の集りで、濕原特有の植物群落あり、夏ならば千紫萬紅のお花畑で緋毛氈を敷きつめた様な美觀を呈する。

沼に題す
Lakes and marshes.

LAKES KIRIKOMI AND KARIKOMI
切込湖及刈込湖

MARSH SUGANUMA
菅沼

MARSH MARUNUMA
丸沼

MARSH KINUNUMA
鬼怒沼

THE HOT SPRINGS

The hot springs, *Funsento, Kawamata-Onsen, Hatchoyu*, etc., on the way from *Yumoto* to Lake *Kinu* through the *Nishizawa* Gold Mine, give something soft and tender to the beauty of the inner Nikko.

Funsento, "the Hot Spring Tower," is a white incrustation tower to be seen here and there over the cliffs along the spring valley. It is made of carbonate of lime and sulphur, and has a hole in the centre from which the hot water shoots several feet up. The tower is of a conical shape, the outside being soft powders congealed, but the years make it higher and harder. It was found only 20 years ago by Dr. *Watanabe*, and is now protected by the state.

The Kawamata Hot Spring lies about fourteen miles from the gold mine, and still has an oldish inn from of old. Lying on the River *Kinu*, it has a charm of simplicity peculiar to such a sequestered corner.

Still going up along the *Kinu*, you will come to **the Nikkozawa Hot Spring.** Water being richer, visitors never cease to come.

Hatcho-no-yu is a hot pool conducted from the cliff behind, where the hot water gushes. The rustic simplicity will attract you.

NIKKO NATIONAL PARK

湯の香慕ひて

湯元から西澤金山を經て鬼怒沼に向ふ途中、噴泉塔・川俣溫泉・八丁湯等の溫泉郷は壯大な奧日光の景觀中でも柔かい感じをもつ一面である。

噴泉塔は湯澤谿谷の斷崖所々に散在する高さ二三尺許りの白色塔で、いづれも炭酸石灰に少量の硫黃を含んだもの、其中央に穴があつて湯を七八尺まで噴出してゐる。塔狀は圓錐形で外皮は柔軟な粉末の凝結したもので、歲月の經過するまゝ次第に硬く且つ高くなる。此の噴泉塔は明治の末頃、東京帝國大學敎授工學博士渡邊渡氏が發見、今日では天然記念物として保護されてゐる。

川俣溫泉は西澤金山より三里、今猶昔ながらに一軒の古風な宿であり、鬼怒川の溪流に臨み、上流約十一里粟山郷の最も奧にある幽邃境、旅舍の名は淸湧館、泉質は弱鹽類泉及び硫黃泉で原始的な趣がある。

更に鬼怒川を遡ること三里餘にある八丁の湯は小溫泉プールで、背後の巖壁から湧出る湯を瀧に引き注ぐ所に野趣があり、淸泉に浸つてゐると旅の疲れが解消される。また日光澤溫泉の泉質は川俣溫泉と殆ど同質であるが、泉量甚だ豐饒、婦人病に奇效ありといふので四時浴客に賑つてゐる。

THE FAIRYLAND

The way from Lake *Kinu* to **Ose** is what is called the roof way, running about twelve miles along the mountain peaks, about 7,000 feet high, bordering the prefectures *Tochigi* and *Gumma*, then *Fukushima* and *Gumma*.

Ose is a name given to the basin consisting of *Osegahara* (plain) and Lake *Ose*, which was caused by the eruption of Mt. *Hiuchi*, whose lava had thwarted and blocked up the valley. Lakes, swamps, woods, dry grass-land, and high mountains make up the beauty of Ose, peculiar to such a table land.

Mt. Hiuchi is 2,346 metres high, and is, so to speak, the king of *Ose* with its magnificent figure of a volcano.

After passing the **Hiuchi Shrine** and over the swamp, if you take a way up the mountain, you will soon get to the top. There on a craggy top, you can have a glorious sight of mountain ranges after ranges extending like waves and Lake *Ose* among them, silent but shining like a big eye of a Titan.

Passing a few swamps from *Numajiri* and going down along the River *Numajiri*, you will come to *Osegahara*, the highest swamp in Japan, 1,398 metres high, with the width of two and one mile each side. It is a narrow basin, surrounded by Mts. *Hiuchi*, *Shibutsu* and *Keizuru* on three sides, and extending into broader **Shobudaira**, "the Iris Plain," to the south. It is belted here and there by the long groves of birches and beech-trees. It is indeed a fairyland.

NIKKO NATIONAL PARK

神秘の仙境

鬼怒沼から尾瀬への道は、栃木・群馬及福島・新潟の國境山脈、約七千尺内外の所謂、尾根傳ひ、五里に亙る縱走林道である。尾瀬とは燧嶽噴火當時の熔岩が、溪谷を阻んで成立つた尾瀬沼・尾瀬原の介在する裕間盆地を指すので、湖沼と、濕原と、森林と、乾燥草原と、高山との交響節奏するところに尾瀬の生命がある。燧嶽は海拔二三四六米、火山型の豪壯な姿で尾瀬一圓に君臨してゐる。

沼尻に立つ焰嶽神社の鳥居をくゞつて裾野の濕地を登り、濕地の盡くるところナデックボの峻坂で、上るに從ひ展望が開け、やがて灌木林の絶頂に達して、巖頭に立てば脚下には尾瀬沼が藍を湛へて沈默を守り、五百重なす周圍の群山は波濤の如く千里に聯る。沼尻から一二の小濕原を横ぎり、沼尻川の谿谷について下ること一里餘で尾瀬ケ原に達する。東西一里餘、南北十八町、海拔一三九八米、本洲第一の高濕原で、東には燧嶽が遠く裾野を延べ、西には至佛山が燧と相對し、北には景鶴聳え、南には菖蒲平一帯がつらなって細長い盆地を作り、これらの中央を白樺山毛欅の巨木が帯のやうに緩やかに續いてゐる。それは沼尻・ヨツビ兩川が貫流する兩岸の樹木で周圍の山はいづれも潤葉樹である。

神秋の仙境
The fairy land.

MARSH OSENUMA FROM MT. HIUCHI
燧岳より尾瀬沼

MT. HIUCHI FROM OSENUMA
尾瀬沼よりの燧岳

MT. SHIBUTSU FROM OSE-GA-HARA
尾瀬ヶ原よりの至佛山

MT. HIUCHI FROM OSE-GA-HARA
尾瀬ヶ原よりの燧岳な望む

THE OSE-GA-HARA
尾瀬ヶ原

MT. HIUCHI FROM SHOBU-DAIRA
菖蒲平よりの燧岳

IF WINTER COMES

ikko prides itself on the beauty of ancient structures, yet if winter comes, a modern spectacle will be presented there; for, since the winter sports, such as ski-ing and skating, came to be popular in our country, the neighbourhood of *Chuzenji* has become one of the most famous places **for ski-ing and skating.**

The *Nantai* Ski Ground is one. It is a very good ground both for beginners and experts, because it is full of variety and the snow is quite good in quality as well as quite deep, and to make the matter better, it can be reached by a few minutes' walk from *Chugushi* Station, which means that even a Tokyo man can enjoy several hours of ski-ing there and go home in a day. Besides, however hard a snow storm may blow, it is quite safe there. And above all, it has the great advantage of accommodating hundreds of people beautiful hotels of perfect equipment. **The ski-ing olimpiad,** held every year on the National Foundation Day in February, is quite well-known and entices all the ski-ing experts of the country.

The view of the *Nasuno* plain with country houses bound in snow, the wind-like ski-ers sliding on the snow, the cheerful skaters over the mirror-like lake, and the exoticism of foreign young beauties skating in the hotel-rinks,—all these must be the attractions to every sportsman.

NIKKO NATIONAL PARK

冬來りなば

古代建築の豪華を誇る日光にも冬來りなば其處には突如として近代的な風景が現出する。ウインター・スポーツとしてのスキーやスケートが最近冬の運動競技界の王座を占めて以來、中禪寺附近は絶好の**スキー場**であり、又**スケートリンク**として有名となつた。

男體スキー場の特色は何れも變化に富み、練習に適し、妙技を揮ふには絶好のコンデションにある。又、雪深く併も雪質が優れ、剩（アマツサ）へ中宮祠驛から徒歩で二分乃至五分といふ交通の便に惠まれ、東京を朝出發すると日歸りで優に七八時間は滑れるといふ便利さに加へて、いかに吹雪が劇しくともこゝばかりは安全地帯であり、その上に數百人を收容し得る設備の完全な大旅館が傍に控へてゐるなど他に類例のない優越さを有つてゐる。毎年二月の紀元節に行はれる二荒山神社の**スキー祭**には湯元のスキー場と共に、あらゆる競技が行はれるので全國のスキーヤが賑々しく參集する。

雪上に競ふスキー、スケート場の明朗にして新鮮なる感覺、わけてもホテルに特設のスケートリンクなどに在留外人のスマートな姿に異國情調をも滿喫させる。

FRAGRANCE IN THE SACRED REGION

he natural gardens of alpine flora blooming in the plateaus on the Nikko Mountain Range must look like the oases or the Gardens of Eden for the mountaineers and arrest their feet as well as their eyes. Mts. *Taro* and *Shirané* are crowned with these more than others. **Mt. Taro,** for example, is the hardest among the Nikko mountains for you to climb; it is full of so steep slopes that you can hardly have time to breathe; and yet what a feast is spread before you after the laborious conquer! For lo! there in the old crater is a grand round bed of flowers—flowers of every kind and colour—bellflowers, gentian, shortia, crowfoot, rhododendron, black lily, mandarin orange, etc.—and the antiqueness of the crater walls around the bed, and the suffocating fragrance coming from these flowers! It might as well be called a sacred region. It is indeed the very garden of a fairy queen.

The flower beds on **Mt. Shirané** are quite unique and another attraction. Every kind of alpine flora in their full bloom adorn the whole range of the plateau, and even the gaps among the piled-up crags and rocks are no exception. And the traces of mountain deer can sometimes be found upon the sandy ground among the flowers. And the season of **Yashu-azareas** also must not be missed by the alpinists.

NIKKO NATIONAL PARK

聖域に香る

日光群峰中、聖域に香る**お花畑**の美觀は一名物として登山者の足を停めさせるに十分だ、中にも太郎山や**白根山**には隨所にこのお花畑が展開され、たとへば太郎山などは登山者からすれば、日光群峰中第一番の苦手といつてよいほど險しさが連續的で息をつく暇もないが、喘ぎ續けてやうやく火山口に立つた時の嬉しさ、其處は實に圓狀いお誂へ向きの花壇だ、平坦な砂原の全部がお花畑で百花妍を競ふ**高山植物**の風情は、まるで御伽噺にでもありさうな王宮の庭園だ、この大花壇の背景として立つ高い火口壁は、太古の面影を見せて聖域といふ感が深い。

お花畑には石楠花・クロユリ・コマクサ・チョウノスケソウ・オヤマリンドウ・ゴゼンタチバナ・ミヤマダイコンソウ・ナンキンコザクラ・イハカヾミなど文字通りに千紫萬紅の美しさで、歩くさへ勿體ないほど咲き匂つてゐる。白根山のお花畑も又天下一品の稱があり、多種多様の高山植物が所嫌はず、巖の列んだ重なつた間隙でも、到るところ妍を競つて咲き誇り、花の間の露はな砂地には點々と鹿の足跡が見えるなど、太古の姿そのまゝだ。尚、此地方一帶に錦を飾る野州花の滿開も見逃せない美觀である。

聖域に香る

Fragrance in the holy land.

THE GORGE

he gorge of the River Kinu is called the "*Yabakei in Kwanto*," owing to the grandness and the secluded calmness of its scenery. The river range is abundant in the natural beauties of water and mountains; here the stagnant water deep and blue with the high precipice hanging over it, and there the craggy mountains steep and high with the commanding nobleness. It is never inferior to the famous Chipi Gorge in China. It is indeed the great mysterious work of art elaborately chiselled by the Creator.

The river originates from Lake *Kinu*, 7,000 feet high, among the Nikko mountains, and runs down nearly thirty miles, irrigating the hot-spring resorts such as *Kawamata*, *Kawaji*, *Taki*, etc., as far as a village called *Funau* where it joins the River *Daiya*.

If you want to know the real beauty of the inner Nikko, you must come as far as the River *Kinu* and see the mysterious phenomenons such as plateaus, lakes, cataracts, rapids, and the deep abyss there, all caused by the erosive actions of water.

The plate shows **Nagadoro,** The Long Gorge, with clear and deep water and steep cliffs, near the *Kinugawa* Spa. The back-water of the river dammed by the *Nakaiwa* Power Station makes a long pool extending about three miles as far as *Tateiwa*, and is called *Kinu Doro*. It is the calmest and most secluded nook in the whole valley. Here you can enjoy yourself in reading, boating, angling, or shooting, seeing the maple-leaves in autumn and the snow scenery in winter.

NIKKO NATIONAL PARK

蒼水淙々

所謂關東耶馬溪の稱ある**鬼怒川谿谷**の幽邃にして壯大なる、由來、鬼怒川流域は到る處山容水態の見るべきもの多く、其天惠に富むこと寧ろ驚くべきものがあり、しかも山岳美と溪流美の粹を蒐めたること、まことに蒼水淙々として竆まるところを知らず、彼の赤壁をして三舍を避けしむるに足る。この天賦の大自然美は造物主が最も意匠を凝らした神秘境で、其源は標高七千尺、日光連峰中の**鬼怒沼**に起り、川俣・川治附近の温泉場を經て、大谷川と合流する船生村の南端まで十有餘里にわたる一大幽谷は古代、噴火後の侵蝕作用のもたらした現象によつて高原・湖沼・瀑布・急湍・深淵等の奇勝を生み出したもので、奧日光の眞の美を探らんとせば遠く茲に鬼怒川まで杖を曳かねばならぬ。

圖は斷崖の脚下碧潭深く澄む温泉附近の**長瀞**で、中岩發電所堰堤に遮られた鬼怒川本流のバックウオータ―は、楯岩(タテイハ)の下流まで、里餘にわたり長き湖水をなすところ鬼怒瀞(キヌドロ)と稱され、舟を浮べて俗腸を洗ふに足るべく、谿谷中第一の靜寂な幽境で、奇岩怪石の布置も面白く、萬年橋の危く中天にかゝる態、或は兩岸に變現する水の形態など、**觀楓・釣魚・舟遊(シウイウ)・狩獵・雪見**等四季の風趣を集めてゐる。

NAGADORO (A LONG GORGE)
NEAR KINUGAWA HOT-SPRINGS
鬼怒川温泉附近の長瀞

蒼水淳々
The Deep water.

THE CHARM OF THE SPA

The hotels in **the Kinugawa Spa** are now not the hut-like inns of old days, but two or three storeyed buildings, with spacious rooms equipped in modern style. They are built upon a high cliff over the bank of the river, with mountains at their back, so that the visitors, sitting in their own rooms, can feast their eyes freely with this grand scenery.

Near the river springs abundance of mineral water, over forty degrees in temperature, which is drawn up above the cliff a hundred feet high and supplied to the hotels, where you can freely take a bath. But more interesting will be the **Cave Bath** near the river, or the natural bath on the river bed, or Sennin-buro, a hot water pool, constructed artificially. In summer, you will swim in the dammed water of the *Kinu* and then rest in one of these baths. And in the evening you can enjoy in it the beauty of a full moon rising among the pine-trees on the cliff or listen to the sonorous songs of miller's-thumbs calling in the near-by river. Kindness and cleanliness are the motto of the hotels which have recently formed a trade guild among them and unified the charges of hotel, lunch, etc. You can fully and peacefully appreciate the hot spring in the nook secluded far from the madding crowd of towns and cities.

NIKKO NATIONAL PARK

泉郷の王座

鬼怒川温泉郷の旅館は今日では小屋がけの昔とは異つて、新装の二階建・三階建の旅館が堂々と軒を並べ、客室も手廣くなつて設備萬端も整つてゐる。

これらの**旅館**はいづれも鬼怒川岸の岩壁上に秀麗な山岳を背景とし、坐しながら雄大壯麗な風光に接することができる。温泉はいづれも湧出量が豐富で温度も四十度以上で、河床から百尺の崖上に温泉を引揚げ、**内湯・貸切湯・林間瀧の湯**等を設け、晝夜を分たず入浴が白山となつてゐる。或は河床湧出口で岩石を其儘浴槽とした岩窟の湯や、河床の天然浴場とし、又は河敷の廣大な區割に人工を施して千人風呂を設けるなど、夏期、鬼怒の清流に泳ぎ直ちに之等の浴槽でその疲れを醫すなど、全く別天地に遊ぶ感があり、又は**天然浴槽**に浸つては斷崖の老松から洩れ出づる名月を賞する(シンシン)など、時には又、可憐な河鹿の美音に心身を澄ます等到底都人士の想像だにも及ばない快事である。

旅館は清潔本位・親切第一を標語として懇切丁寧、最近温泉組合の組織成り、宿料・中食料其他諸物價に至るまで統一され、輕佻な都會風を排して家族的な温泉氣分を發揮せしめる所、仙郷の生命であり王座をなす所以であらう。

泉郷の王座
The throne of the spa.

THE GENERAL VIEW OF KINUGAWA HOT-SPRINGS
鬼怒川温泉全景

THE GENERAL VIEW OF KINUGAWA HOTEL
鬼怒川ホテル全景

ROWING IN THE CLEAR STREAM

he Gorge of the River *Kinu* is another fairyland remote from the madding crowd's ignoble strife; the quietness of this sequestered corner will surely prolong the life of visitors there.

About 200 metres from *Kosagoé* Station, and you will come to **a suspended bridge,** more than 200 feet long and 52 feet above the river water, built ten years ago at 13,000 yen. It is suspended by a steel wire tied to the iron tower on each side the river, the elasticity of the wire equal to 474 tons. The water under the bridge is 30 feet deep, and beautifully reflects the trees, flowers, tinted leaves and the snow, according to the seasons. Besides, the fantastic rocks and stones add to the beauty of the scene. It is a place very good for sight-seeing, boating and angling throughout the year.

The Nakaiwa Bridge, 55 metres distant from *Nakaiwa* Station, consists of twin bridges built upon a rock and the banks more than 60 feet high. It is quite an attraction.

The waterfall **Otaki** hangs in the main stream about 400 metres up the river from *Yunotaki*. It thunders down, splashing water all around among the fantastic rocks on the banks. It is worthy of the name, "the Big Fall."

You can also have a distant view of Mt. *Takahara* towering nobly into the cloud from the *Kinugawa* Spa; the fantastic sight under the *Kurogane* Bridge has no pararell.

NIKKO NATIONAL PARK

清流に漕ぐ

鬼怒川溪谷はまつたく俗塵を超越した仙境で、其浮世ばなれのした靜寂さは觀光客に數年の壽命を延ばさせる。

中岩橋は中岩驛より半丁、六十餘尺の岩上に二連の橋渠を架したところ、正に天下の奇觀である。小佐越驛より二丁にして小佐越吊橋の奇觀に接する。鬼怒川の中空にかゝる鐵線の吊橋は大正十四年、工費一萬三千圓を投じ架設したもので、長さ二百三十尺、幅六尺、水面よりの高さ五十二尺、釣線の彈力四百七十四噸といふ素晴らしいものであるが、一名萬年橋とも云ひ、鋼鐵線と鐵塔をもつて高く層崖に懸り、橋下の水深三丈、鬼怒の碧潭に兩岸の樹影を映して、花に、若葉に、紅葉に、四季とりぐゝの美觀は形容に詞なく、加ふるに奇岩怪石起伏して一層の風致を添へ、觀楓に、舟遊に、釣魚に好適地とされてゐる。

鬼怒川溫泉大瀧は湯の瀧の上流約四町の本流中にあり、奇巖怪石兩崖に聳峙し、飛湍の狀物凄く、水聲轟々、水沫四邊に散亂して濃霧を起すところ、大瀧の名に背かぬ一大壯觀である。其他鬼怒川溫泉より遙か野州の西北部に方り、秀然として雲表に聳ゆる高原山の雄大なる遠望、又、くろがね橋下の景觀の如き、天下無比と云つて過言でない。

EVER SURPRISED

A. A grand sight of Tateiwa

If you go down half a mile along the bank of the *Kinu* from *Kinugawa-Onsen* Station, you will find that the rapid stream, making a curve, slows down into a deep abyss, near which on a dry bed towers a big rock called *Tateiwa*, "the Shield Rock," about 200 feet high and forty feet wide, the centre projecting higher so that it looks just like a shield; hence the name. It is indeed a wonderful sight.

B. The Nijimi Fall

The *Nijimi-no-taki*, "The Rainbow-Viewing Fall," hangs on the east bank of the river, about a mile north along the road from *Shin-Fujiwara* Station. It is about 60 feet high, dashing against the rocks with such vigorousness that the mist, reflecting the sun, makes a beautiful rainbow; hence the name.

C. A grotesque sight of Usagihané.

If you still go up half a mile from the *Nijimi* Fall, you will notice big rocks standing one after another for about a mile on the bank of the river, the width of which becomes narrower and narrower until it comes to the narrowest point, only about ten feet wide, so that even a hare can jump across it; hence the name *Usagihané*, "the Hare-Jumping."

D. Goko-iwa.

Gokoiwa, "the Five Coloured Rock," lies a quarter mile from *Usagihané* down the river. It is a huge rock with such a big hole in the centre eroded by water that it can hold fifty men in it. When the setting sun shines aslant into this cave, the cave-walls present a pretty sight of five colours; hence the name.

E. Kawadoko-Onsen

I shall have no need of retelling about *Kawadoko-Onsen*, "The River Bed Hot Spring," a natural bath made on the river bed of the *Kinu*, whose rural beauty one can never forget.

NIKKO NATIONAL PARK

迎接に違なく

鬼怒川温泉楯岩の壯觀

鬼怒川温泉驛より鬼怒川の西岸下流約十丁、渓流の屈曲して激流忽ち深淵となり、其の一方の磧に屹然と聳ゆる巨巖を楯岩と稱へる、高さ恰も二十丈、幅四五十尺、巖の中央部が突起して楯に似てゐるので此の名のある所以、正に天下の奇觀として珍重されてゐる。

虹見瀧

新藤原驛より街道上を北に十町、鬼怒川東岸にあり、直下六十餘尺、落下する水の物凄さ、水煙の漲るところ陽に映じて虹となるので此名がある。

兎跳ねの奇勝

虹見瀧の上流約十町進めば本流兩岸の巨巖迫つて起伏すること十數丁、其最も狹い處を「兎跳ネ」と稱し、潤さ僅かに丈餘に過ぎず、野兎もよく跳び得るといふので此名がある。

五光岩

兎跳ネの下流四五町の東岸にあり、急流の浸蝕著しいため巨巖に空虛を生じたもの、高さ四十尺、五十人を容るゝに足る、落日が斜に洞口から岩壁に映ずる時、五色の美觀を呈するので此名がある。鬼怒川瀞峽の絶勝として天然浴槽川床温泉の野趣は前に逑べた通りで玆に事新らしく説くまでもあるまい。

THE AUTUMN TINTS IN A FAIRYLAND

he Kawaji Spa, the best among the hot springs along the River *Kinu*, might be called a fairyland, with its pretty sights of the hanging bridge, *Sengandake*, etc.

The hotel *Ohmiya Kawaji Kwan*, which has the sole possession of the hot-springs, is about 5 miles from *Shin-Fujiwara* Station on the *Shimozuke* Electric Railway, and 15 miles from *Taun* with the facility of tram-cars, coaches and buses. It has a family-bath and a cave-bath, and gives the guests the freedom of cooking their own meals.

Gohanseki, "The Seal Stone," one of the attractions in this fairyland, stands in the main stream of the River *Ojika*, two miles up from the spa. It is thirty feet high above the water, and is also called *Musubi-ishi*, "A Rice-Ball Stone." In the ancient time when they settled the borders of three feudalities, *Nikko, Utsunomiya and Aizu*, they signed or sealed the documents on this big stone; hence the name.

The *Kawaji Spa* has the family-bath, the reserved bath, the water-falling bath in the grove, etc., but the cave bath and the river bed bath are the most attractive because of their rural simplicity. They are quite primitive. *Komochi-no-yu*, "the Child Having Spring," for instance, is a natural pool walled in by rocks around, and in autumn it reflects the pretty tints of maple leaves on it. It is indeed a paradise on earth. It is said that a woman never fails to conceive a child, if she bathes in this spring; hence the name.

NIKKO NATIONAL PARK

仙境に彩る

鬼怒川渓谷温泉中の白眉である川治温泉は川治吊橋や仙巌岳の景勝を控へて風光絶佳の仙境である。此温泉場は下野電鐵新藤原驛から二里、今市よりは六里で電車・馬車・乘合自動車の便があり、浴場は家族湯と岩窟の湯でいづれも自炊の設備がある。この仙境を彩る**御判石**は川治温泉より上流へ三十丁、男鹿川の本流中にあり、水面より突出すること三十尺餘、一名握飯石とも稱へ、その昔、日光神領と會津宇津宮の二藩三領土の境界線として議定書を決した時、此石の上で押板したのが御判石と云ふ始まりである。

川治温泉場の温泉は内湯・貸切湯・林間瀧の湯等、いづれも詩情豊かな風景であるが、中にも最も野趣に富んでゐるのは、河床の湧出口で天然の岩石をそのまゝ浴槽とした**岩窟の湯**や、**河床天然浴場**である。この天然浴場などは全く原始的で、野趣満々として掬すべきものがあり、たとへば「**子持の湯**」などはその代表的なもので、四面は累々たる岩石をもって蔽はれその中に天然のプールをなしてゐるので、清らかな湯に浸つて遙か山峡の紅葉などを心ゆくまで眺めてゐるとそのまゝに地上天國の樂土である。字義通り子寶を授る靈泉で婦人病に特効がある。

A DISTANT-VIEW OF KAWAJI HOT-SPRINGS
川治温泉の遠望

仙境に彩る
Tints in the fairy land.

GOHAN-ISHI, KAWAJI HOT-SPRING
川治温泉御判石

THE BATH HOUSE, KAWAJI HOT-SPRINGS
川治温泉浴場

A NATURAL BATH
天然風呂

昭和十年二月二十日印刷
昭和十年三月 十日發行

不許複製

編輯兼發行者　柏田長七
宇都宮市馬場町三二〇八番地

印刷所　下野美術工藝社
宇都宮市馬場町三二〇八番地
電話三三八八番

發行所　星野屋分店
栃木縣日光町
電話二五七番

■解説
エハガキ店星野屋
誕生から終焉まで

卯木 伸男

宇都宮をはじめ日光、那須など、栃木県内を写す絵葉書の多くに、写真説明とあわせて「星野屋」の名前が印刷されている。その表示は、「明神下星野屋製」、「明神下星野屋支店発行」「馬場町大通星野屋製」とさまざまであるが、それはすべて宇都宮二荒山神社参道石段下に戦前まで店を構えた絵葉書問屋星野屋を指すことに相違ない。

星野屋の初代柏田長七は、一八八五(明治十八)年に和歌山で生まれ、横浜の絵葉書業「星野屋」で修業。外国人に好まれた江ノ島、藤沢、鎌倉、小田原、箱根など湘南地方の風景絵葉書を手がけていたという。

当時の時代背景をたどれば、一九〇〇(明治三十三)年九月十七日に逓信省が私製絵葉書の制定を告示、写真や図案を用いた絵葉書の発行が容易になったことから絵葉書業が生業として成立していったものと考えられる。

長七はその後、星野屋から暖簾分をもらい、日光、那須、鬼怒川、川治など栃木県内の観光地絵葉書を作るために来宇。「星野屋商店」の屋号で、一九〇五(明治三十八)年ごろ二荒山神社前に店を構え、絵葉書製造に乗りだした。星野屋は、撮影から封筒の意匠、印刷、販売まで一貫して行い、県内全域

宇都宮に星野屋を設立した柏田長七

に販路を拡大。ホテルの宣伝用絵葉書や、第十四師団など軍関係の記念絵葉書も手がけた。『北関東の中枢 宇都宮の景観』(十六枚組)と題された封筒の裏側には、「宇都宮市伝馬町星野屋印刷部」とあり、分店日光の電話番号とともに、取扱品目として「美術印刷一般・エハガキ製作・各種アルバム・額縁額装・便箋封筒・トランプ花札」と記されている。

また、星野屋の特徴として絵葉書表面の切手貼付場所に、星印にKの文字が白抜きされていた。

今に残る「明神前」を写した絵葉書の左側に、『エハガキ』星野屋支店』の丸い看板と、絵葉書が並べられた陳列台を見ることができ、往時の商いぶりがしのばれる。のちに星野屋は大通り沿いに洋風三階建ての店舗を出店した。看板にタバコ、パイプの文字が見えることから、喫煙具など絵葉書以外に、幅広い商品を取り扱っていたことがうかがえる。

明治期から大正期にかけて作られた絵葉書は、コロタイプ印刷が用いられていた。この印刷方式は、約百五十年前にフランスで生まれた技術で、資料「コロタイプの製版と印刷の実際」(山口須美)を要約すれば、「ガラス版を刷版に使用することから、かつては『瑠璃版』と呼ばれ、撮影・製版・印刷と大変手間のかかるものだった。しかし、連続階調による滑らかで深みのある質感や印刷に和・洋紙を選ばない特製や耐久性の高いインキとの融合によってできる、印刷表現は他に勝るものだった」。

日本にコロタイプ印刷が導入されたのは、一八八三(明治十六)年内閣印刷局が始めといわれ、一八八九(明治二十二)年には、東京深川で東京印刷会社が創業した。星野屋商店が明治後期にこれら機材一式と技術力をもって、自前の絵葉書印刷工場を宇都宮に設立したこ

花咲く明治時代後期の二荒山神社参道と、エハガキ店星野屋の店先

中禅寺湖に浮かぶ帆船（オフセット印刷）

柏田長七は、一九二九（昭和四）年に日光町下鉢石に星野屋分店と日の丸写真館を設立。日光を中心に中禅寺湖、湯元、鬼怒川温泉方面に機材を背負い、自転車、リヤカーで撮影に出かけている。一九三五（昭和十）年には、和英訳『国立公園 日光の展望』を出版。ちなみにその一部を紹介してみる。「今の日光見物はスピードに恵まれている。参道はバスに乗って……快適な速度で飛ばし……そして訪ね行く先々の面白き愉快さ。金谷ホテルから望めば山麓の彼方に帯一筋、大谷川の清流が白く光る。遙かに聳ゆる群峰は朝霧に模糊たり」。小書は日光の魅力を余すとこなく紹介した今でいう写真ガイドで、その迫力は見る者を唸らせる。

長七はその五年後、一九四〇（昭和十五）年八月二十五日、肺結核を患い他界。五十五歳の若さでこの世を去った。当時、使用していた機材、フィルムとも宇都宮空襲ですべて壊滅。残念ながら現存する物は何もない。

とは、時代の最先端を担っていた証左に違いない。

また、当時の彩色（カラー）絵葉書は、墨刷りの絵葉書に、人工的に一枚一枚手彩色したもので、大正期にはいると大量生産ができるオフセット印刷に代わっていった。彩色絵葉書は、関東大震災で終焉を迎えたといわれる。

昭和初期の大通り。右端の洋風三階建てが星野屋エハガキ店

資料提供：有限会社アイシークリエーション一級建築士事務所　柏田 健介氏
解説文は、宇都宮商工会議所「天地人」に連載した「一枚の絵葉書から 石井敏夫コレクションより」を再掲したものである。

柏田　健介 ［かしわだ けんすけ］
1967年宇都宮市生まれ。
2003年有限会社アイシークリエーション一級建築士事務所を設立。
現在、同社代表取締役。
明治から昭和（戦前）にかけて、栃木県内を写す絵葉書を多数製造するとともに、本復刻版の原本『國立公園　日光の展望』の発行所である「星野屋商店」店主柏田長七の曾孫、好吉の孫にあたる。曾祖父の業績を後世に伝えるため本書の出版を企画した。
座右の銘は、「正しく古いものは永遠に新しい」

解説　卯木　伸男 ［うき のぶお］
1958年宇都宮生まれ。長野大学卒業後、印刷会社勤務を経て1985年編集工房随想舎を設立。以来、出版と編集制作を業務に栃木県をテーマとした出版活動を行う。著書に『絵葉書が映す下野の明治・大正・昭和—石井敏夫絵葉書コレクションより』（随想舎）がある。現在、有限会社随想舎取締役社長。

復刻版　國立公園 日光の展望

2015年5月15日　第1刷発行

柏田　健介［編］

発行所	有限会社　随 想 舎	〒320-0033　宇都宮市本町10-3　TSビル TEL 028 (616) 6605　FAX 028 (616) 6607 振替 00360-0-36984 URL http://www.zuisousha.co.jp/ E-Mail info@zuisousha.co.jp
印　刷	株式会社シナノパブリッシングプレス	
装　丁	栄舞工房	

定価はカバーに表示してあります／乱丁・落丁はお取りかえいたします
ⓒKensuke Kashiwada 2015 Printed in Japan　ISBN978-4-88748-306-4